Please Don't Feed the Seagulls

...and Other Vacation Mishaps

Amber N. Black

Text Copyright © 2025 by Amber N. Black

2nd Edition

All rights reserved.

No portion of this book may be reproduced in any form without written permission from the publisher or author, except as permitted by U.S. copyright law.

For privacy reasons, some names, locations, and dates may have been changed or omitted.

Book Cover by Cody Michael Mahurin.

Contents

Dedication	V
Disclaimer	VII
Introduction	IX
Prologue	1
1. St. Pete Beach, FL	7
2. Washington D.C.	15
3. The Bran-sun	23
4. Las Vegas, NV	29
5. Nashville, TN	37
6. The First Cruise	43
7. Memphis, TN	57
8. The Bahamas	67
9. Chicago, IL	77
10. Wisconsin Dells, WI	87

11.	Close to Home	103
12.	Southern Caribbean Cruise	113
13.	Caribbean Cruise: Girls Only	121
14.	The Forgotten Cruise	131
15.	Central Colorado	141
16.	Southern Caribbean Cruise 2.0	159
17.	The Last Cruise	173
18.	Amarillo, TX	183
19.	Southern Utah	193
20.	Blue Ridge Mountains, North Carolina	203
21.	Maui, HI	211
22.	Gatlinburg, TN	227
23.	St. Louis, MO	239
Epilogue		247
Acknowledgements		249

For my family, for making all of these adventures possible.
Here's to many more.

and

For Katie.

Disclaimer

Here we go, the start of the vacation adventure and vacation disasters. Now, I have taken other vacations besides the ones you will read about; however, I've tried to include the ones I remember most, the vacations with the most excitement, the most blunders, and the most comedy attached.

Every mishap in this book is real, while dialogue and other minor details may be enhanced, the book and events themselves are real. Some adventures in this book should be either avoided or attempted at your own risk.

This book includes a real-life family that none of this would be possible without. While their memories may differ from mine, I wrote the book, so we are going to go with how I remember it.

For anonymity some names have been changed or omitted.

Introduction

Think of your favorite vacation.

What does it look like?

A beach?

The mountains?

Maybe it was a weekend home alone while your significant other is away? Maybe it was the time you took your kids to Disney World, or the girls trip you took on a long weekend? For the adventure types, maybe it was an overnight camping trip, or the week spent at the hunting cabin?

What made it your favorite? Was it because you had never been to that destination before? Or because of the company (or lack thereof) you had? Maybe it had nothing to do with the people or the place, maybe it was just a feeling, something inside your soul. Just a feeling you knew, that this wonderful moment would leave a mark on you, somewhere deep, that you just could not quite get over.

Did you try something new? Did you find a new love for something or someone? Was it your favorite because everything went according to plan? Perfect weather, perfect place, perfect itinerary. Everything went off without a hitch, no disagreements, everyone got along, and you came back safe and sound. Because that's the most important thing, right? That everything goes perfectly?

The perfect vacation is the best vacation, right?

Right?

Not necessarily....

A vacation can have a multitude of different meanings.

A weekend trip to the city for some, a long getaway to a country vineyard for others. A luxurious five-star hotel in the Swiss Alps, or even the Motel 6 at the closest tourist trap. A husband on a 3-day hunting trip, that is a vacation, and the wife home alone for those 3 days, is also a vacation. Sometimes a vacation is just a week or a couple of days off work where one can sit at home and do what they want when they want, *Friends* reruns in your bloomers eating a whole bag of pizza rolls... or so I've heard.

Disney World, a cruise in the Caribbean, the beach, the mountains, camping, backpacking, road trips and staycations, all are some of the best ways to relax, unwind, adventure, and make memories. My family and I have dabbled in quite a few of those.

For some families, a vacation brings up many special memories. For our family it brings memories alright, good ones, unexpected ones, and the exciting ones. Ones that make me think *'that was so fun, I am so blessed'* and other memories that make me wonder *'How. Are. We. Still. Alive.?'*

Shipwrecks, water rescues, and getting lost and injured are just some of the few "special memories" that we have had on our family vacations. I hope that this book gives you not only ideas of things to do and see in some of these places, but also a warning of what hilariously bad things can go wrong.

Don't call this a guidebook to vacation. I don't want to be held responsible for someone's vacations to include some of the moments like mine.

INTRODUCTION

Sure, I'll give you suggestions and tell you my favorite places and adventures to try, but proceed at your own risk.

Do, though, let it be a reminder that sometimes the most fun and the most exciting things about vacations are the disasters, the getting lost, the random changes that must be made. Family vacation doesn't have to be perfect, that would be boring. Life is not perfect so why should your adventures be? In my opinion the only thing you have to have for a great vacation, is family, friends, and a sense of humor.

Be curious, be adventurous, laugh when you want to cry and cry when you laugh.

Because Life and Adventure can be *SO EXCITING,* if you let it.

Prologue

The First Vacation

It's late at night. A single mother pulls off Highway 44 to a crusty gas station. Her 10-year-old daughter asleep in the car. She pulls up to the pay phone, inserts a few coins and dials.

"Dad, it's me Terri, yes we're ok. We made it to St. James." She says trying not to let the exhaustion and nervousness show in her voice.

"Yes, the tire is holding up so far."

She listens as he gives her instructions.

"Okay, yeah, we will call you when we get to Steelville... Ok, yes, about thirty minutes... okay... Love you too."

That is how the first family vacation went. I personally wasn't there but this story was told to me by my mother and sister, it happened about 4 years before I was born.

The first vacation. The best vacation. So, I'm told.

The first ever family vacation was to Branson, Missouri. A major tourist town in southwest Missouri. It's near the Missouri, Oklahoma, Arkansas conjunction and welcomes families from all over the world. Home to attractions of many kinds, from singing and magic shows to water and amusement parks, there is something for everyone in Branson.

My Mom, after hard work and determination, saved up enough money to take her and my sister on their first ever family vacation, just the two of them.

"It was the best vacation!" My Mom tells me with as much excitement in her voice now as the day they left.

Like reading your favorite book for the first time or seeing your favorite musician live for the first time, that excitement, that feeling, and thrill can never be repeated in the same way.

Growing up, in a family of seven in a single income household, and then as a teenage mother with a new baby and a job in the factory, vacations were not a thing. Hard earned money was not spent on vacations. After hard work, determination and grit, and a realization one day while making baby bottles at the local factory, this was not the life for her, so Mom changed all of that.

She worked hard, got a nursing degree, worked any shift in any hospital department, and saved up that very, very hard-earned money to take herself and my sister on their first ever family vacation.

"We planned and planned. And saved and saved. We wrote a letter to the welcome center of Branson and anxiously awaited a reply. We finally got our tourist packet in the mail. A big manilla envelope full of brochures and magazines. Because in 1985 we couldn't research on the internet like we could today. We poured over those pamphlets, picking out what hotel we were going to stay at and picked out what fun things we were going to do. We of course picked a hotel with a pool and water slide. I meticulously planned

how much money I would need for each day and made sure we didn't go over budget."

"Now, we had it all planned out, money wise and time wise what we were going to do. And we did just that. Whitewater, Silver Dollar City, Shepard of the Hills, we did it all. We had the best time. So, on the last day of our trip we had it planned out to a T. We were going to check out of our hotel and spend the entire day at the waterpark, Whitewater! From the time they opened we spent the entire wonderful day riding waterslides and floating the lazy river. We didn't leave until almost closing time.

"I had $50 left to get home. Fifty dollars to get from Branson, Missouri to home, 4 hours and 230 miles. So, we're on the stretch of highway between Branson and Springfield, and that's when I get a flat tire. We hadn't been driving an hour. I got out of the car, it was a Wednesday night, church night, so I got out and told Lisa to stay in the car, I couldn't let her out on the side of the highway while I was trying to figure out what I was going to do.

"While I was surveying the situation an older couple on their way to church, probably the same age your grandpa and grandma were at the time, stopped behind me. Thankfully it wasn't some "creeper" pulling over, I wholeheartedly believe God sent that couple to me, To help me. The man changed the tire and put the spare on for me, wanting nothing in return and sent us on our way.

"I limped down the highway with three tires and one donut spare all the way to Springfield so I could call dad and tell him what had happened. Well, he didn't like the idea of us coming all the way back home on a spare, he told

ME I NEEDED TO FIND SOMEWHERE TO GET A REAL TIRE. SO ONCE AGAIN, BY GOD'S GRACE, I FOUND A TIRE SHOP THAT WAS STILL OPEN, AND FOR $35 THEY PUT ME A TIRE ON, INSTEAD OF THE "DONUT" TIRE.

"I CALLED DAD BACK AND TOLD HIM I WAS ABLE TO GET THE TIRE REPLACED. HE WAS GLAD BUT STILL WORRIED, SO HE SAID TO HEAD ON HOME, BUT TO FIND A PAYPHONE IN LEBANON AND CALL HIM WHEN WE GOT THERE, WHICH WAS ABOUT AN HOUR AWAY.

"WE GOT TO LEBANON, I PULLED OFF, FOUND A PAYPHONE, AND PARKED VERY CLOSE SO WHERE I COULD STILL SEE LISA. I CALLED DAD, I COULD HEAR HIS MAP RATTLING IN THE BACKGROUND AS HE LOOKED AT IT AND SAID TO CALL HIM AT THIS PLACE AND THIS PLACE, NAMING OFF ALL THE TOWNS I WAS SUPPOSED TO STOP AND FIND A PAYPHONE. AND I DID. I STOPPED AT EACH AND EVERY EXIT HE TOLD ME TO CALL HIM FROM. OUR LAST STOP BEFORE WE MADE IT HOME WAS POTOSI, SO I STOPPED AND CALLED, AND HE SAID 'GREAT! CALL ME WHEN YOU GET HOME!'

"WOULDN'T YOU KNOW IT, I WAS SO HAPPY TO BE HOME AND OUT OF THAT CAR, I FORGOT TO CALL HIM WHEN WE GOT HOME!"

The first vacation didn't go without a slip, but that didn't change status as "The Best Vacation". Ask Mom or Lisa today and they will tell you how much fun they had, and of the blunder of the flat tire. Their facial expressions and excitement in their voices won't change with either part of the story. I recently asked Lisa to tell me about this vacation, what she remembered. She didn't even mention the flat tire! All she remembers was how exciting it was for her and Mom! From the planning to the waterpark, it was such a fun vacation for both of them.

The flat tire was not the bad guy of the story, it is simply part of the story. The first vacation wouldn't be the adventure it was without that hiccup. It simply made it more interesting and exciting.

So, if the next few chapters do anything, I hope it's that they prove that the best vacations don't equal perfect vacations. Problems of all kinds have weaved their way into our many, many family trips. And I speak for all of us when I say we would do them a million times over and have just as much fun and laugh just as hard as the first time. It's a vacation, it's meant to be FUN!

Chapter 1
St. Pete Beach, FL

This is the year our family vacation grew to include myself and my nephew Brenden. He was two and I was thirteen at the time. This is going to be his first beach trip and for the both of us it was the first time on an airplane. We flew from St. Louis, which is about an hour drive from our hometown, to Tampa, which was only about a 30-minute or so drive to our final destination of St. Pete Beach, Florida.

Lisa, my sister, is an Ultrasound Tech. and that year the hospital she was working at was sending her to Florida to learn echocardiograms, which is a fancy ultrasound of the heart. Mom and I tagged along for the ride, to watch Brenden, and as a bonus we were rewarded for our babysitting duties with a beach vacation . If Lisa had known how the babysitting would play out, she may not have accepted our volunteer work.

This was my first plane ride. I was thirteen at the time and surprisingly had no fear of flying, especially since my current 35-year-old self gets super stressed out right before a flight. It sounded like an adventure back then though. What also makes this surprising is because this trip and first flight came not long after the tragedy of 9/11. A day that most Americans can say they remember everything about. Like the bombing of Pearl Harbor and assassination of JFK, that day, September 11th, is burned into our memory. Anyone who remembers watching two planes crash directly into a couple of skyscrapers has the right to be a little anxious when it comes to flying, even if you only watched on television from the safety of a 7th grade history class.

Airport security got a major overhaul after 9/11. The banned items list grew, the security checkpoint is way more involved, and no more seeing your family off at the gate. Everyone knows all items go in the x-ray bin, including cell phones and shoes, no matter if you are 2 or 82, shoes in the bin.

The shoes. The shoes in the bin is where our first trauma on this vacation starts. You want to know how to completely ruin a two-year old's day, make him take his Spiderman light up shoes off for TSA. Now, in his defense he did have a 101° fever, I'd be pretty crabby too if my entire body was on fire. However, his anger about the shoes just got funnier and funnier. Because it was no longer about the shoes, it was life that he was mad about. Mad at life and mad about being at the airport and not somewhere else he had in mind. Other than the kicking and screaming and crying, his words were...

"I just wanna go back to Desloge!!!" Brenden said with tears running down his red cheeks flushed with fever. "Just take me back to Desloge!" Which actually sounded more like "dewoge" because his Ls sounded like Ws at that age.

Now, to those of you wandering *"what's a Desloge?"* It is a small town not far from where we live. It's a nice little town, it's got the closest Walmart, and, at the time, it only had one stoplight. No, we do not live there. Aside from Mom and Lisa 30 years ago, none of us has had a Desloge address including this said screaming two-year-old. Why he chose that to be his safe haven from the hell hole that was Lambert Airport is a mystery to us all, including him.

Now, I know what you are thinking. A two plus hour flight with a sick screaming kid sounds like exactly zero fun for everyone involved including the other 150 passengers. But like most kids, a switch was flipped when the Spidey shoes went back on and the only thing he wanted to know was "When's this thing gonna blast off??".

This statement caused a bit of panic for Mom and Lisa. In a post 9/11 world you do not talk about things blasting on a plane! Certain things are banned to discuss in certain places, you don't talk about how quiet it is in a hospital or when the last time you got a speeding ticket was. On a plane you don't say things like blast off, or that the left phalange is missing. (If you know, you know) Thankfully, other than the select few sitting near us, we were the only ones that heard him.

If you've never flown into Tampa, it is a trip. If you get your seats on the, we'll call it the "good side", it will look just like you are about to fly directly into the Tampa Bay. At one point you can look out your window and see nothing but water. The blue coastal waters being the only thing filling your tiny oval shaped window. Quite a startling scene at first, but if you let yourself enjoy it, it is a very cool view. If the thought of that terrifies you, hopefully you are seated on the other side.

St. Pete's Beach is a great little coastal town. It is on a barrier island, or island that runs parallel to the mainland of Florida, and it's within driving distance to other larger coastal favorites like Clearwater, St. Petersburg, and Tampa. We had plenty of places to eat and shop. I was introduced to the wonderful world of coconut shrimp, which you will learn later is an absolute favorite of mine, in a story my sister's kids love to bring up. But that's for a later chapter.

There was a Walgreens close by, and when you are traveling with a sick kiddo you need a convenience store handy. Somehow, after that first night stocking up on Tylenol and Motrin at the Walgreen's we managed to go to that same Walgreen's every night of our vacation.

Every. Single. Night.

Done adventuring for the day? Let's go to Walgreen's.

Want to go shopping for souvenirs? Let's go to Walgreen's.

Just simply don't have anything else to do. You got it. We are going to Walgreen's!

I'm not sure what it was about the Walgreen's in Florida that we were so obsessed with. It could have been the convenience of it or the fact that we didn't have one within a 30-minute drive back in Missouri. Whatever it was, we were known by first name at that location by the end of the week. Something I'm sure everyone brags about when they get home from a trip.

I wonder what Walgreen's Betty is up to these days.

This trip included a lot of firsts for us. First flight, first beach vacation, first taste of delicious coconut shrimp, but also first dolphin sighting, first sailboat trip, which included our first brush with death on our vacations, and first-time learning about seagulls, which included our second brush with death on vacation.

I get it, you're probably thinking that sailing, yes, obviously is a dangerous sport, sailboat accidents happen all the time. But how does a seagull encounter end up being dangerous and years later causing PTSD to a 23-year-old grown man? We'll get to that.

One of our big adventures we took on that vacation, other than the 13 trips to Walgreen's, was a sailboat tour around the Bay where your chances of seeing dolphins were pretty high. Lisa was at class, so Mom, Brenden, and I loaded up in the rental and headed out for a nice relaxing sailboat trip to hopefully see dolphins. Wrong. That sailing trip was in no way peaceful, calm, relaxing or any other happy words. The side of our boat was in the water more than the actual hull of the boat. The deck remained at a steep 45° angle the majority of the trip. Ropes everywhere, salty water splashing in our faces, I can't see where we are going or if we are sinking, we've all just got blind faith in these strangers that we are still afloat.

We don't live near an ocean, so maybe that's a norm when sailing, I don't know. Mom was so terrified of Brenden falling off the boat however, she couldn't enjoy any of it. Frankly neither did I. I assume she was worried about me too; I was only 13 but Brenden is the first grandkid, so he probably ranks higher than I do on some "nonexistent" list. Parents have favorites, don't deny it, we all know it's true.

We did see dolphins though, I'm fairly certain they were laughing and judging us as they swam past, but technically the trip was a success.

Dolphins: check.

Still alive: Check.

Now, seagulls. We've all seen seagulls. Whether in real life or on tv, oceans and seagulls are always seen together, walking on the beach or gently gliding in the ocean air breeze. Their cute little black and white bodies pecking gently at the sand or swooping down to the water, in search of a crab or fish. You can't help but notice when you go to the ocean or the beach, you see seagulls.

What you may not notice on the beach is a sign, in big bold black letters, that says, "DO NOT FEED THE SEAGULLS". We certainly didn't see it as Mom, two-year-old Brenden, and I decided to share our fries with the feathered friends. At first it was no big deal, throw a fry in the sand, watch a gull come take it and fly off, repeat. Then like some kind of oceanic horror movie, with gulls instead of crows, swarms of them start circling us, plunging toward us, more and more just swooping and diving for the fries. They came so close as to steal the food right out of our containers! Brenden was traumatized. Hands above his head, screaming. Mom and I don't know what to do! Eventually we just chucked the containers said "you can keep the burgers too", Mom grabbed Brenden, and we took off for the car.

Some guy stopped us when we got to the car and asked "Didn't you guys see the sign? You really shouldn't feed the seagulls; they get kind of vicious."

Yeah. Noted. Thanks.

To this day, even as a 23-year-old college football player, Brenden still has PTSD about the seagulls. If we are walking on any beach, he gives them a wide berth and we are not even allowed to joke about them. Just recently we were in Gulf Shores, and he starts yelling at his sister, because she was joking about the seagulls walking past our chairs. "Hey, look Brenden, it's your friends!" she says. Smirking, slightly giggling, knowing full well how he feels about the little birds.

"Seagulls are no joke, Emily! You don't know!"

One of our last nights in town we went out to eat at what felt like a fancy restaurant, I don't remember much about it, maybe it was my small-town roots that made me think it was fancy, who knows. There is one major thing about this meal that will forever be a highlight, and it didn't even happen in the restaurant. Before you get the check at most any restaurant, the waiter always asks some version of "did we leave room for dessert?". I would venture a guess that 90% of the time it's a no. It was this time too, except they had key lime pie. If you've never had key lime pie, it's like a chilled cheesecake with lime and whipped cream on a graham cracker crust. *Magnifico.*

Anyway, we were all full, so we got our said key lime pie to go. We make our way back to the hotel, for relaxing, enjoying the ocean view, and getting the last few things together for our drive to Orlando the next day. Suddenly, I hear Lisa bust out laughing so hard she probably peed herself. I turn around to see my mother, the matriarch of our family, with a look of 'oh crap they caught me' while she holds the entire piece of pie in her hands having it halfway shoved in her mouth! Filling smeared on her lips. Pie crust sprinkled on the hotel bed.

"What?" she said, graham cracker crust scattering the hotel bed as she spoke "They didn't give me a fork?"

Chapter 2
Washington D.C.

My freshman year of high school, the school marching band was selected to play in a parade celebrating the opening of the World War 2 Memorial in Washington D.C. Yes, I was in the marching band, call me a nerd if you like. Anyway, DC is about 870 miles from my high school, we rode the whole 14 hours of it on a charter bus. Not the same charter bus mind you because of course we broke down somewhere in Pennsylvania. We had to wait for a replacement stuck at a McDonalds, for hours. That is how this wonderful field trip started.

Washington D.C. Our nation's capital and home to dozens of monuments and memorials to honor our nation's history. This particular weekend, the city held a parade and a four-day celebration, in dedication to the men and women who served and lost their lives during WW2. Now, while our marching band was chosen to play in the parade ceremony, I was not. I was given the task of holding a banner. I could tell you that I volunteered to hold the banner to introduce our band to the nation's capital, but it was probably more likely that I was a terrible clarinet player, and therefore chosen to hold the banner instead of playing an instrument. Either way I still got to go to Washington D.C. and loved every minute. The first-person people saw from the Raider Regiment, was me! Well, me and the other member who was holding the opposite end of this massive banner. I'm sure she really did volunteer because she was actually good at playing an instrument, I just wanted something to do and a trip to D.C.

Lisa did not go on this trip, instead it was Mom and my cousin Laura. They made the multi-state drive together, traipsing through Illinois, Indiana, Ohio, Pennsylvania, and finally Maryland. They, however, did not break down on the way and did not have to spend lunch and dinner with the red and yellow clown. Imagine the torture of having dozens on dozens of sweaty snarky teenagers stuck in the same sweaty smelly fast-food joint for hours on end. Thank God my mother was taking me home, I don't think I could bear another bus breakdown. And from what the unlucky souls whose parents couldn't take them home told me, the bus did breakdown again, and they had to endure the last few states with a lovely smell of sewage coming from the onboard lavatory.

Thank you, Mom, you truly are my hero.

We finally make it to DC. The school and probably many of the parents arranged for us to visit a lot of historic sites. Something I probably didn't appreciate enough while there. We visited Lincoln Memorial, the Korean War Memorial, newly constructed WW2 Memorial, and the Vietnam War Memorial. All are equally somber and humbling experiences. If you ever get the chance to visit DC, add these to the list, all are remarkably well built and do a fantastic job memorializing the men and women who gave their lives for our country.

Other staples of D.C. that we got to visit were The Reflecting Pool, Washington Monument, and the Smithsonian, which contained all kinds of history like ruby slippers from the *Wizard of Oz*, uniforms from the All-American Girls Baseball League, and so much more.

The dedication to the WW2 Memorial included a some speakers, a parade, and lots of guests. There were crowds of people everywhere. Many of which were wearing their veteran's apparel, leather vests adorned with many patches of their respected squadrons, and the military hats embossed with "Korea War Vet", "WW2 Veteran", or the ships that they or their sons and daughters sailed on. A prominent sighting on these vests, hats, and even flags was the initials P.O.W M.I.A. Which if you aren't familiar stands for "Prisoner of War, Missing in Action". It's black in color with white lettering and a silhouette. It is designed to remind us that some of our nation's warriors are still missing.

Laura was not familiar with said flag.

"What's all this powmia about?" she asked, as if it was all one word.

"What powmia??" Mom asked, looking at me, who was just as confused.

"All these black flags with powmia. Who is powmia??"

To this day almost 20 years later I cannot see a P.O.W M.I.A flag and not think about '*who is powmia?*'. Laughing but trying not to make Laura feel like an idiot we explain what P.O.W.M.I.A stands for and she bursts into tears with laughter. We all three got a huge kick out of the confusion and knew that this was going to be a great trip.

When the parade was over, Mom signed me out of the school's custody, and I spent the remainder of the trip, and the ride home back to Missouri, with her and Laura. The three of us spent the last day checking out some other sights, but our main goal was to find one particular memorial that meant something special to us.

We took the subway a few times, and once was approached by a man selling maps to the city for five dollars. This was perfect. This was a time when google maps and smartphones were not around or not as widespread anyway, the smartest thing my little Nokia could do was play *Snake*. So, we bought this perfectly timed salesman's map to downtown Washington DC, I mean "it's only $5", talk about a steal! We get not even a block down the street with our new fancy map, and wouldn't you know it, we notice this steal of a deal $5 map says "provided free by Marriott Hotels" on the back.

Yeah, talk about a steal alright.

On our walk, with our new map that some homeless man okey-doked us with, we made our way past the J. Edgar Hoover Building and the US Navy Memorial Plaza and finally to what the three of us had been looking for.

***

On September 30, 2001, Steven 'Chachi' Ziegler, passed away in a freak car accident on the main highway in my hometown. Steve was a sheriff deputy for St. Francois County, and he was also our cousin. The memorial Mom, Laura and I wanted to make sure we visited was the National Law Enforcement Officers Memorial. It's made of curving marble walls and it is etched with the names of officers killed in the line of duty, like Steve. It's a heart wrenching thing seeing a member of your family, enshrined in a memorial at our nation's capital, we are grateful for his bravery and service but miss him dearly. The day of his accident, like 9/11, is a day that our family and most of our community will never forget. Laura being blessed with the family genes of writing, came up with a short poem on the spot. So, we left flowers and a small American flag with the poem that reads...

WASHINGTON D.C.

"2 years have passed since that sad and dreadful day.
The roses are in remembrance of you,
This flag for the service that you gave. We love you. – Amber, Teresa, Laura"

We left the roses and did a few stone rubbings of his name to take home, and we left, a little sad but grateful for the experience.

***

Fortunately, or unfortunately, however you want to look at it, our trip home was just as eventful as our trek there. We didn't have to endure riding in a car with sewage smell, but it was just as exciting. Highway 76 is also called the Pennsylvania Turnpike. Wall-to-wall traffic going over 70mph and concrete barriers on both sides of the lane, Mom, in the driver's seat at the time, looked like she was driving Bolivia's Death Road. She was white knuckled and about two inches from the steering wheel the majority of the time on the turnpike.

"Mom relax!" "Teresa get off the steering wheel!" Two sentences that were repeated so many times on that highway, Laura and I finally just gave up and let Mom look like a 92-year-old who was trying to see over the wheel of her Cadillac.

Somewhere in Ohio, maybe Columbus maybe Cleveland, we decided to call it a night. We finally found a sign indicating hotels at the next exit, and we make our way toward where the lovely blue lodging signs were pointing so we could finally get some sleep.

We notice the entire parking lot is filled with police, EMS and other emergency vehicles. Already committed to the turn we head into the parking lot. We immediately get stopped by one of the friendly looking officers.

"We were wanting to get a room for the night, is there a problem at the hotel?" Mom asks hoping for just a pulled fire alarm, or some kind of false alarm. Not something that's going to get us on the morning news.

"Oh, we just had a little robbery in the hotel but if you give us an hour or so I'm sure you can get a room after we get this all situated." The officer explains so nonchalant. This is an everyday occurrence in the area by the sound of his tone.

Ha! No thanks!

We'll take our chances in some other town.

Once again, this trip was taken before everyone had a smartphone and Google Maps at their fingertips. We took this entire trip with printed maps from MapQuest and TOMTOM GPS. We drove down a few streets looking for somewhere else to sleep with no luck, the TOMTOM yelling at us for every turn we made. The tiny GPS so inconvenienced by our need for rest. Sleep is not on the schedule for TOMTOM. Eventually we got completely lost and ended up running a red light in what looked to be a very sketchy part of town. Unsurprisingly Mom, so flabbergasted by the whole situation, runs another one. Apparently two is the limit on running red lights in Ohio. Naturally, we're pulled over and got to speak to our second Ohio law officer of the night. What a roll we were on.

Mom and Laura explained the situation, while I sat in the back seat wondering if one of us was going to end up in jail by the end of the trip.

With utter concern or extreme surprise that we had somehow gotten so lost that we ended up in the ghetto, he let us off with just a warning and urged us to get out of the area immediately.

"Make a left at the next street, get back on the highway, and find a different exit to get a hotel!"

The next street we were instructed to turn on: Broad Street.

Yup, sounds fitting for three lost broads.

CHAPTER 3
THE BRAN-SUN

Most people think that traveling with a toddler is too much. It's too stressful. They won't remember it anyway.

Well, let me tell you, sometimes it's worth it. The stress, the cost, it's worth it. Maybe they won't remember everything about it when they get older, but you will, and you can enjoy all the ups and downs in those memories. All the ups. All the downs.

Branson, Missouri. We touched on this earlier, but just to refresh. Branson is a top vacation destination in my home state, possibly even the country. It was even mentioned in the movie *She's Out of My League*. Home to so many entertainment theaters, including singers, magicians, and Dolly Parton's Dixie Stampede (as it was known previously, now it's just Dolly Parton's Stampede). Outlet malls, a giant Bass Pro Shop, Silver Dollar City, Shepard of the Hills, Ride the Ducks, all are just a few of the must-see attractions of this place.

With Branson being fairly close to where I live, we have visited quite a few times. I say fairly close, but it is still a 4-hour drive. I can get to my mother's new home in Kentucky faster than I can get to the other side of my own state, but that's Missouri for you.

Once, I went to Branson with my best friend Katie and her family when we were in high school. I think that may have been the first time I had been on a vacation without either of my parents or my sister. Silver Dollar City was our main goal for that trip. It was in November, so the entire park was dressed up for Christmas. Silver Dollar City is an amusement park and a step back in time all rolled into one. You can go straight from the Fire-in-the-Hole roller coaster to a blacksmiths booth and watch someone pound away shaping something that a power tool has replaced long ago. There are many homestead attractions and other roller coaster rides, shops, old log cabins and churches, and of course food vendors.

Katie and I had a blast, as teenagers do, we said see you later to the parents and headed for the roller coasters. November was a perfect time to go. We weren't freezing yet but it was cold enough to keep the crowds down. We'd finish a ride and see that the line was empty, so they'd let us go another round without getting off. What I wouldn't give to be 17 again and riding The Wildfire four times in a row with my best friend.

Another time, the summer of '04, my sister was pregnant with my niece, and we all decided we needed to have a summer vacation with just the 4 of us, Mom, Lisa, Brenden, and I, and technically my niece Emily too. Em was born in October of that year so she was almost ready to make her appearance by the time we went on this trip.

You always hear that "kids say the darndest things". The randomness that can come from a toddler's mouth is what makes that so true. On our 4-hour drive to Branson, we spend the majority of it on I-44, after a long twisting and winding drive through the country. While on this drive my four-year-old nephew would start randomly saying things like "think outside the bun, DING" and "eat fresh" and "have it your way!". Every time he saw a sign for a fast-food joint, he would start rattling off their slogan! It was hilarious, and he knew it. So, for two more hours, through the peaks and valleys of the Ozark Mountains, after finding out how funny he was, we listened to line after line of slogans.

You may be wondering why this chapter is titled Bran-sun. Well, the little goof with all the commercials memorized, somehow mixed up the Pac Sun clothing company and Branson. So, from the time we left the Pac Sun at the Branson Landing pretty much to this day, Branson has been known as "THE Bran-sun".

Another fun place to visit while you're in Branson is Whitewater. It's got all your classics when it comes to waterparks. Tunnel slides, open air slides, slides with tubes and ones you just slide down on your bum, lazy river, wave pool, Whitewater has it all. Teenagers, like me, and toddlers, like Brenden, love waterparks!

So, obviously Mom and Lisa planned this little adventure just for us to enjoy right? Well, not entirely.

Now, going to the waterpark was definitely for us to enjoy, the excitement and thrill of seeing a kids face light up when they see the giant slides that only exist in dreams is incredible and very fulfilling. However, my then 46-year-old mother was probably more excited than the two of us kids. This woman has not met a waterslide she would not attempt. Even to this day at 60, uh 60....uh we'll just say, even the older she gets she is still all about the waterparks! She is truly one of the most fearless and adventurous women you could ever meet.

Lisa, baby bump in tow, and Brenden, hung out in the kiddy pools while Mom and I got our fill on the big waterslides. This would be about the only time in our lives where I was tall enough for something that Brenden wasn't. At 6'5" he now towers over my lowly 5'2" frame (5'3" with shoes on). Something we "all" get a laugh about. (Insert eyeroll here, no one likes to be the short joke of the family).

We rescued Lisa from the constant 'Mom watch this!', "Mom look!", "Mom watch me!", and took Brenden with us to rip down the smaller, gentler slides. Even a few he snuck on by tippy toeing. I guess we were all having so much fun we didn't realize how long we'd been gone. We go back to find Lisa, being pregnant all she could do was float the lazy river or lay in a beach chair, and she is beat red from the sun. I'm talking tomato. Her pregnant belly was so sunburnt we were certain Emily would already have a summer tan when she made her appearance in a couple months. To this day Emily always gets a great tan in the summer and absolutely loves to be in the sun, maybe that summer has something to do with it.

Before 2018, Ride the Ducks Branson was a very popular tour, it is a land and water tour of the area. Multiple locations around the country, they use amphibious vehicles, nicknamed "ducks", as you can guess because they go on land and water, to tour the city and lakes nearby. The Ducks in Branson, will take you on a tour through the city streets, giving little tidbits and history facts, then change to boat mode and take you on Table Rock Lake.

Unfortunately, and with great sadness in 2018, the tourist attraction had to shut down after one of the vehicles capsized and sank in Table Rock Lake, killing 17 of the 31 souls aboard. I remember seeing the breaking news stories saying that one of the boats had sunk after a fast-approaching storm had taken the area by surprise, causing it to capsize. I had been on that tour a few times and was completely shocked by the tragedy. The fact that a vehicle modeled after a war machine sank was mind blowing.

THE BRAN-SUN

The summer we visited Branson, our Ducks tour went without a hitch. We drove the streets, learned some history, and then floated along Table Rock Lake, they even let Brenden "drive" the boat. We had a great time, that is, until we got back to the dock.

Brenden is my best buddy even though we are ten years apart we are inseparable. That day however, he was not my best buddy. He was being such a little punk after the Ducks ride. I mean a downright devilish brat. Lisa had finally had enough.

She told Mom "Give me the keys to the Jeep!". She grabbed Brenden around the waist, carrying him by her side like a stack of textbooks with her pregnant belly too much in the way to carry him anyway else, and headed outside.

A few minutes later they both come back in, and it was like night and day. Brenden was so pleasant and loving toward me and Mom. No more Chucky impersonations. We never learned what happened out in the Jeep, some kind of exorcism I guess, but we never had any more "come to Jesus meetings" as we call it, the remainder of the trip. But when anyone starts acting like a fool all that's needed is...

"Mom, Give me the keys!"

Chapter 4
Las Vegas, NV

Viva Las Vegas. Sin City.

I was only 16, so not much sinning coming from me, unless you count tiptoeing onto the casino floor just to see what would happen.

"Ma'am! Get the minors off the casino floor!" a statement we heard coming from multiple directions from very angry looking floor people in the Paris Las Vegas Hotel and Casino. Apparently, you are supposed to play "the floor is lava" at all times if your underage in Vegas and whatever you do, DO NOT step on the casino carpet!

This trip was more than just a family get away this time. I doubt many people would pick Vegas as a family destination. This trip included three adults, me (16), my nephew (5), and now my baby niece (5months).

Welcome to the shitshow Emily.

This was actually a destination wedding, Mom was getting remarried and instead of a typical wedding in our hometown, which she has already done. We all went to Vegas!

Mom and my new stepdad, Ed or Edwardo as we call him, left a few days early for their road trip to Vegas. They went through Texas, New Mexico, Arizona, the works, stopping off at a few tourists draws along the way. I stayed with Lisa and we flew out a couple days later. The experience this time in the airport was way more chill. No freak outs over the Spider-man shoes and no "I just want to go back to Desloge!", amazing how much better a mood one can be in with a normal body temperature.

The flight was also uneventful. We couldn't sit with each other, but we weren't far. Baby Em sat on Lisa's lap in one row, Brenden sat with his dad in another, and I was by my lonesome. Netflix was only mail order DVDs at the time so no binge watching on my Razr phone, but I did get to bring Mom's laptop. What do you watch when you are on a 3-hour flight from St. Louis to Vegas? That's right, you watch *Vegas Vacation,* starring Chevy Chase and Beverly D'Angelo. The more I look back and the older I get, I sometimes feel like I am living a real-life *Vacation* movie.

This is Emily's first vacation, and at only 5 months old she remembers exactly none of it today. A baby on any vacation can be stressful, but as far as I remember she was in no way a burden on the trip, except when she almost got us all arrested. That's what I said, the baby almost got us arrested. Okay, so technically it was Brenden and I who almost got us pulled over in the first place, but her mere existence would have definitely gotten someone thrown in jail.

You know on all the shows and movies where someone is driving down the Vegas strip and the person in the back opens the sunroof, they stand up, stick their head through it and take in all the amazing lights and sounds and city atmosphere? The breeze blowing through your hair, the palm trees lining the streets, colors, flashing lights, the fountains, the people, it is all so bright and mesmerizing! There is no way to focus on any one thing, your head is on a swivel the entire time. You don't know where to look, everything catches your eye. But did you know that the police don't actually like when children do that?

Yeah, we didn't either.

We flew into Vegas late at night, super cool by the way, I recommend. Mom and Ed picked us up, after we landed. We got everything loaded in the Jeep, and then realization hits. We forgot a car seat for Emily! We didn't need one for the plane, because she was just going to be held the whole time. Now hers was in the number 3 parking garage at Lambert Airport. Okay, no big deal, someone decided, we can just hold her on the way to the hotel, it's not that far, and then Mom and Ed will go get one in the morning before we start checking out the sights. Problem solved.

On the way to said hotel, we head down the Vegas Strip. Me, having just watched *Vegas Vacation*, remembering the scene where Audrey gets stuck in the sunroof trying to check everything out, has a brilliant idea! The Jeep has a sunroof! So, I make my way toward the front of the car crawling over suitcases and adults holding children and stick my head out. It is exhilarating. It's just like the movies, so many lights, so many buildings, so many sounds! As I've mentioned, Brenden and I were inseparable and of course my little mini-me wants to do everything I do. So, he bolts out of his seatbelt, stands on the console and he is now head and shoulders out of the sunroof waving and cheering, just as captivated by the surroundings as I am.

It's wall to wall traffic on Las Vegas Blvd, cars are barely moving forward let alone changing lanes. Brenden and I are waving and shouting to anyone who will listen, on top of the world. And what do we hear over the traffic, the casino sounds, and the crowds on the street?

"Get the minors in a seatbelt! NOW!!" a police car is behind us, flashing his lights screaming at us through a megaphone! "Get the children inside the vehicle immediately!" Mom and Lisa are slightly panicked. If they manage to get us pulled over, we are so screwed. Lisa is trying to keep Emily out of sight while making sure Brenden doesn't get up again, because not only do we not have a car seat for the 5-month-old, but we also don't have a booster seat for Brenden, who is only 5. Thankfully though, the traffic sucked just enough to keep the adults out of the clink for the night or at the very least a hefty fine. This is the first bit of screaming in our direction we endured on this trip but it certainly won't be the last.

Casinos are abundant in Vegas, obviously. There is a lot for everyone to see though. Most of the big casinos are hotels and shopping centers and restaurants all in one. The *New York, New York* even has a roller coaster in it, complete with a Statue of Liberty replica. *The Paris Las Vegas* has its own Eiffel tower and Arc de Triomphe, plus a giant hot air balloon neon sign filled with lights that you could see from anywhere on the strip. Of course, you cannot go to the Vegas strip without an *Ocean's 11* moment outside the Bellagio. The massive fountain out front puts on a spectacular show and bonus, it's free! *The Venetian* was also a stop we made and even though you are completely inside at this Italian compound of a hotel, the ceiling throughout the mall area looks like a beautiful cornflower blue sky dotted with white clouds.

We, well most of us in our family, are all about trying new things. Local restaurants, sticking your head out of the sunroof when it's illegal, coconut shrimp, death by sailboat, death by seagull, whatever! We are here for it! Well, you know what's something they have in Vegas that they don't have in small town Missouri? Nope not casinos, we've got slot machines in our local grocery store. (No, I'm not kidding.)

It's Oxygen Bars!

Whoever thought of this as an enterprise is a genius. You pay for something that's free all around, but like the small town suckers we are, we (the parents obviously, I had no money) bought it! I have no idea who decide "let's try this out" but somehow, we all agreed, and it was a weird experience but hey, when in Rome right? The little shop is very open, filled with neon lights and bubbles, and these pillars that light up with bubbling water, you feel refreshed just walking in. As the name implies, you sit at a bar, and they give you oxygen, that's basically it, just like at a hospital; plastic tube, two prongs, up the nose. This experience gave me a kickstart of sympathy for those who have to wear oxygen just to live. I spent less than 30 minutes with that tube tickling my nose hairs and I will never do it again unless medically necessary. I don't think any of us felt refreshed from the boost of oxygen, we had headaches and dried out sinus cavities. Nose bleeds aside at least we can say we tried it. It doesn't make the list of do overs, though.

The best part was this other contraption they had. Ever been to a car wash? Ever gotten a massage? Well, the tanning bed looking situation they had at the Oxygen Bar did just that. You could lay in this, "bed" if you will, that was somewhere between a coffin and a tanning bed, and it would give you a back massage with power sprayers. And you know with Mom getting remarried and thinking someone was getting carted off to jail as soon as we got to Vegas, I had a lot of stress, I somehow convinced Mom that I definitely needed a carwash back massage! Now this I would do again!

Were those experiences kind of weird? Yes. Did they still add to the adventure as a whole? Yes. Don't ever be afraid to try new things. Even if they are on the strange side.

A must see if you are in the Vegas area is the ever-monumental Hoover Dam. Built in the 1930s it was once the tallest dam in the United States, but it now will have to settle for second place after the Oroville Dam in California passed it up in the 1960s. Even if you are not a history buff or fan of architecture, I promise it is worth a visit. Its sheer monstrous size will have you in awe. It's 4.4 million cubic yards of concrete and creates a water reservoir, Lake Mead, almost 29 million acre-feet of water. Watch *Vegas Vacation* first though, it will make the experience that much better.

It is a great time just checking out the huge structure, looking down to see how afraid of heights you are, and checking out the cool blue waters of Lake Mead. You can even pull a *Walk to Remember* moment, in the scene where Jamie wants to be in two places at once, so Landon takes her to the state line. That's possible on the Hoover Dam as well, it is split almost equally in half by the Arizona/Nevada state line. Two places at once: check!

As I have mentioned, my in-flight entertainment was the movie *Vegas Vacation*. In the movie the whole fam heads to the Hoover Dam for a dam tour. And that's what gets repeated over and over. Dam.

"We're going on a Dam tour."

"Take all the Dam pictures you want."

"Are there any Dam questions?"

"Where can I get some Dam bait?!"

Best part, they really do call it a Dam Tour. Of course, my 16-year-old self loved that. Who am I kidding, 35-year-old me does too. When you get a chance to swear in front of your parents and not get in trouble, you can feel pretty untouchable. It's like swear words somehow put you on a whole other level of coolness. I've already mentioned my nerdiness, move along.

"The car is in the Dam parking garage." I would say. "Let's get some Dam snacks."

My mini-me, Brenden, was all about it too. He looks on in amazement that I'm not getting in the slightest bit of trouble with all this swearing. Like our parents have lost their hearing, or we are in a land with no rules. So, he pipes right in too.

"We gotta walk to the Dam building?" he said confidently waiting for repercussions. Since he didn't get any, mostly just some snickers and laughs from me, because who can deny how cute it is when kids cuss. "Mom let's get the Dam stroller! So, we can take a Dam Walk."

That last comment pushed our luck a little too far, with Mom and Lisa giving me a look like it was my fault he said those things. They were right, it was my fault. What kind of auntie would I be if I didn't talk him in to cussing. Even at 35 I still con my nieces and nephews into using their best sailor lingo. My newest nephew, Briggs, likes to throw a cuss word out there every now and again and it takes everything I have not to even crack a smile, or we will both be in trouble.

My advice, if you want special treatment at the Hoover Dam, bring a stroller. We had a tour guide that took his job very seriously. Like secret service serious. Directing people where to sit in the theater for the documentary, he looks directly at the seven of us shouting, (I warned there would be more yelling), shouting very sternly at that "STROLLER FAMILY! Right here!!" pointing at us, waving his hands and side radio to a couple of front row benches like he's landing a 747. Multiple times on this tour we are referred to as "The Stroller Family", like we've taken on the name of our new adopted family. "Stroller Family" first, this way and "Stroller Family" to the elevator. Much like the 'Dam Tour', 'The Stroller Family' took on a life of its own.

"Stroller Family to the Jeep!"

"Stroller Family lets go get some supper."

"Stroller Family it's time for a wedding!"

I'm sure since first mentioning that we were on a destination wedding in Vegas, you've been waiting, dreading, and/or hoping it's an Elvis wedding or least some other celebrity impersonator wedding. Sorry to disappoint. It was a normal everyday wedding, or as normal as any wedding can be in Vegas.

Mom and Ed chose a quaint little building that looks just like a small country church called 'The Little White Chapel' for their nuptials. Which "coincidentally" is their last name. White. That's right, my last name is Black, and my mother's is White, that is not a typo. Everyone at my high school, and really to this day, gets a big kick out of our last names as well.

Just recently, my mother and I had to give our names in a checkout line. The cashier looks at us, deadpan, not amused at all "What is this, Clue?" then turning to my sister, "Are you Colonel Mustard?" I guess she thought we were screwing with her.

The wedding itself goes off without a hitch. Ed in a tux, Mom in a dress, and the rest of us in our Sunday best. Mom is so happy, and if she is happy, we are happy. Having your parents be married to anyone besides each other can cause some uneasy feelings, but this seems to be working out just fine. We grab all the essential photo ops after the wedding, and we change clothes in the chapel, because no one wants to walk around the desert in their Sunday church clothes. Then we head to the car and another adventure. Halfway to the car, walking across the drive-thru wedding lane, is where the last bit of yelling comes in…

"Hey!! We're trying to get married here! Get out!!" the couple at the drive-thru starts shouting and berating us, through the car window, complete with a couple middle fingers, like we just barged in like a group of wedding crashers to their very 'private' ceremony.

Sorry we interrupted your special day folks, in the drive-thru!

Chapter 5
Nashville, TN

Nashville. Music City. Home to sports teams, the famous Broadway Street, bars and Honkey Tonks, Country Music Hall of Fame, countless celebrities, and of course The Grand Ole Opry.

Less than a five-hour drive from home time mostly spent on an interstate highway, the trip can be easily made for us. We've been a multitude of times for concerts, vacations, sporting events, or a day trip. It's also less than a two-hour drive from mom's new home in Kentucky.

My first trip to Music City was a high school graduation present from my sister Lisa. The 5 of us; Lisa, her husband, Brenden, Emily, and I, took an extended weekend trip to Tennessee's capitol to celebrate the year of 2007 and my inching into adulthood. This trip is what started the now ongoing tradition of taking the high school graduate on a trip of their choice as their gift. It is my favorite family tradition by far!

We stayed at the Gaylord Opryland Resort. It has got to be one of the most unique hotels I have ever been to, and I've been a lot of places. With an amazing glass ceiling, it is the perfect atmosphere for the Garden Conservatory inside the massive building. Waterfalls, buildings inside buildings, and so much greenery, like an oasis that if you didn't know for sure, you would think you're in some magical town tucked in a jungle. This 'little' gem is located away from downtown but still in the city, within walking distance of the Opry Mills and The Grand Ole Opry itself.

Part of the present included a trip to both. Shopping and dining at the Mills and a concert at the Opry! I am no stranger to country music. Most that grow up outside city limits find more country on their radios than anything else. My family, however, has a little more stock in country music. "Arkansas" by the Wilburn Brothers, "I haven't seen Mary in Years" by Mel Tillis, "Brewster's Farm" by Porter Wagoner, and so many others were written by my grandpa, Damon Black, or just "Pa" as we called him.

Many others in my family have the gift of music, whether writing, or composing, or singing, or playing an instrument. My great-aunt Sharon wrote songs for Lorretta Lynn, Mel Tillis, and others. My dad, Dave, has written many songs and plays multiple instruments, my brother Josh can do the same. So many of my cousins and aunts and uncles play or sing, in church or in a band or just at home. So much talent in one family that it's unfair. Unfair, because I got nothing! Nothing! Not even a hint of that gene crossed my DNA, the inside of my car can attest to that, the poor thing.

But nonetheless, country music still holds a special place in my heart, so when Lisa said we were going to see one of the biggest names in country, I was ecstatic. Mr. Hotter than a Hoochie Coochie himself! Mr. Alan Jackson! Front row balcony with a perfect view of the famous stage, we sang along to his songs all night!

I will forever be on the team of "spend your money on memories, not things". Graduation, Christmas, birthdays, you name it, for me and my family time together somewhere outside our home address will always be better than boxes with paper and ribbon.

That brings me to one of my favorite "gifts" we've ever given. Also, in Nashville.

My niece's 13th birthday was approaching and Ed Sheeran was coming to St. Louis. Lisa and I decided this would be the perfect gift! We all three love Ed Sheeran, and what 13-year-old wouldn't want a night in downtown, singing along with one of the world's biggest stars! However, with too much procrastination and the fact that neither of us make doctor money, we didn't get tickets for St. Louis. Which actually worked out in our favor because multiple concerts in the Lou were canceled that year, including Ed, because of "safety concerns" due to many protests happening in the city. Thankfully, Nashville was also hosting everyone's favorite red head, that isn't named Weasley, for a couple of nights.

Tickets bought, route planned, bags packed, time off work, all that's left was to surprise the kid. Some people give you the line "oh, I hate surprises" but secretly they love every second of it because it's all about them! Well, this particular teenager said she hates surprises, and she meant it.

There are two kinds of people in this world when it comes to road trips. One you can say to them you're going on a trip, they say ok, and ask what time to be in the truck. The other, you can say the same thing and is a game of 52 card pickup with all the questions being thrown at you, rapid fire, no breath in-between, and most of them repeated.

"Where are we going?"

"When are we leaving?"

"How long does it take to get there?"

"What states are we going through to get there?"

"Where are we going?"

"Whose car are we taking?"

"Will it be hot?"

"What do I need to pack?"

"Do I need a jacket?"

"What are we driving?"

"Who all is going?"

"What are we going to do when we get there?"

"Who all is going?"

"Where are we going again?"

"WHERE ARE WE GOING!?!"

Emily is that second one. The poor kid was in agony the entire four-and-a-half-hour drive. Still in her volleyball uniform and pads, she's in the back of the truck sweaty and miserable because "why won't you just tell me!?". Every couple of hours in-between cat naps and being so irritated with us she's not speaking to us, we would get some version of "where are we going?".

Surprises aren't for everyone.

She figures out that Nashville is the final stop. We get checked in to the hotel, still not telling her about the last part of the birthday present, tell her to put on something nicer than a sweaty jersey because we are going to go "check out the sights". The three of us put on our favorite jeans and tee shirt (you can take the girl out of the smalltown but not the smalltown out of the girl), and head for Downtown. Em, the whole time, was thinking that this was the big surprise, a trip to Nashville for the weekend. *Au contraire* little one. We take her to outside the Bridgestone Arena to see what the huge crowd was all about. I get my phone out just in time to get the best reaction on video!

The realization on her face, a look of wanting it to be true but being afraid we were going to tell her it's not, was priceless. As annoyed as she was with us on the way, she was even more so excited that this was the big surprise. Even strangers on the street were so excited for her when they realized it was all a big surprise. It is my most favorite trip to the Music City. The happiness on her face was the best part of that trip.

That and watching Lisa "run" down the corridor in a leg cast because she almost missed Sheeran's opening song. Step-thunk-step-thunk-step-thunk-step-thunk-step-thunk-step-thunk.

"Mom! Hurry up! Music is starting!!"

"I'm trying Em! You try running in this thing!" step-thunk-step-thunk-step-thunk.

Four and a half hours to get here, and you picked now to go pee?

Chapter 6
The First Cruise

"**WHY DID YOU LET US SLEEP UNTIL 4PM!?!?!?**"
That is how I was loudly welcomed back into my state room on the *Carnival Elation* by my best friends, Katie and Dan.

By the way it was 10am, not anywhere near 4pm.

The winter of 2013, two of my besties, Katie and Dan, and I decided to treat ourselves to a Caribbean cruise to heal some of the winter blues. I was two years post Radiology school and finally making some big kid money, Katie was a senior in college, and Dan was on leave from the Navy. What better way to celebrate someone coming home from a boat in the ocean than making them get on a boat in the ocean. I certainly can't think of anything better.

Katie, having been the only one of us that had been on a cruise before made all of the arrangements. Dan has technically been on a cruise, but it wasn't as much fun, I'm assuming. This one probably has better food, better entertainment, less yelling, and no chance of getting blown up.

Again, assuming.

We went on a five-day cruise on the *Carnival Elation* out of New Orleans, stopping in Progreso and Cozumel, Mexico. It's about a 10-hour drive to get to NOLA, that's what the 'cool' kids from good old southeast Missouri call it, NOLA. It is by far one of the most boring drives one could possibly take. From all my road trips, the only drive that keeps it out of first place for the worst drive ever, is Highway 70 through Kansas. Wow is that awful, but that's another trip for another time.

Ten hours, all but about an hour is spent on the same highway. Interstate 55. For 9 hours straight! Four and a half of those are spent in Mississippi alone. Do you know what there is to look at in Mississippi on a road trip? NOTHING! It's highway, trees, sky, exit signs, that's it. And the exit signs are few and far between. Something we found out the hard way when we needed gas, and I had to pee so unbelievably bad, my eyes were swimming.

This whole trip started on the wrong foot before we even left. Like I said Dan was on leave from the Navy, stationed in Virginia. He was going to be home for Christmas and then we were going to leave for our cruise. At the last minute he wasn't going to be home. Then he was going to be home, but late. By the grace of God, he made it back just in time. Katie and I felt slightly bad for stealing him from his family after he had just gotten home, but only slightly. Sorry Laura.

Now, your boy lives in the middle of nowhere when he's home in Missouri. I mean 30 minutes from any town, take four different gravel roads to get there, cell service only when the wind is right. So, I tell him the night before don't forget anything and especially "do not forget your birth certificate!"

We agree to meet at Katie's parents the next morning around 4 am. If we would have met anywhere else, Katie would have easily been about 6 hours late. She's the type to get in the shower about 3 minutes after you were already supposed to be there. So, meeting at her house was just easier on everyone.

Dan and I arrive at Katie's house at about the same time, he gets out of the car with a look of absolute dread. "Dude." Insert nervous laugh. "I forgot my birth certificate."

Awesome!!

No big deal, we have all day to get there, and the ship doesn't leave until the next day, but we wanted to check out New Orleans first. Better believe we didn't let him off the hook easy. So now it's off to New Orleans, via BFE. It all worked out in the long run. We had over 24 hours until our ship left, but someone decided we'd make up time in the land of no scenery and drive about 90 through the Magnolia State. I won't name names, but it may have been the one that put us behind in the first place, and not Katie because she was ready to go when we got there. Something that shocked everyone involved.

Obvious pro tip, come prepared if you ever go on a long road trip, bring something to occupy the time. Audiobook, regular book, trivia, download a movie, whatever, because after a few hours the radio stations suck, and you will definitely run out of things to talk about. That is unless your name is Katie and you've been stuck at a college in Iowa for four years. She/We had a lot to talk about, and somewhere south of Memphis a rule was implemented that there was no more talking when The Dan was driving. I don't think the guy that can't remember the one thing he was told not to forget had any authority to make rules in my opinion. No worries, welcome to 2013, where unlimited texts are included in your service plan.

Ping.

Giggle. Tick-tick-ticktick-tick.

Ping.

"Haha!!"

Tick-tick-tick-tick-tickticktick.

Ping.

"I know....Oops, I'll be quiet."

Tick-tick-ticktick-tick.

Ping.

"Bahahahaha!!"

Tick-tick-tick-tick-tickticktick.

Ping.

We texted back and forth from the front seat to the back for about 30 minutes before Mr. Rule Maker got so annoyed that the first rule, that we were technically following, got tossed out. We didn't have anything to talk about after that though.

New Orleans at night is a good time. Bourbon Street is loud and gross, and the place to be when in NOLA. The smell. Wow. Beer and vomit and urine are about the only clear smells you can identify coming from that area. As you can imagine, it's a street lined with bars and drunks, but there are plenty of good restaurants and shops too, and don't forget about the jazz and the voodoo.

Now, I am a Christian, and I am right with the Lord, so I don't get freaked out by "supernatural" things, ghost or haunted houses, things of that sort. But a Voodoo house, that is a different level of creepy. It's dark and smoky, and the lady working gave us stares like she was cursing us and our family for merely existing. Think Madam Zeroni from *Holes*. Bones, that I'm hoping are fake, statues that have more jewelry than my Mema Helen, black candles, tarot cards, alligator heads, and so many other things I didn't even know what they were, covered the entire closet sized shop. Plus, the incense that was burning somehow made the vomit and alcohol smell nonexistent, and not in a good way, so that, for sure, is some voodoo magic!

Other than that, Bourbon Street is a blast. We found a restaurant, ok not a restaurant, but a bar that served food. We didn't care we just wanted something that didn't come from a gas station. Like any bar menu, it had burgers, sandwiches, chicken, and a few other things. Unlike most bar menus, however, this place serves a gator burger. Yes, a burger, made of alligator. Fantastic by the way, totally recommend. I was hesitant at first, but Dan insisted we all needed to try it. Here where my love of trying local, unique and/or bizarre foods starts.

You could spit and find a drunk having the best time of their life here. Did you know that you can buy alcohol right on the street? You don't even have to go into the bars to get the party started. Some folks were walking around with hotdog carts, not selling hotdogs, but selling giant beers. And not just a bottle or can or even pitcher, but containers of beer so big it puts 7-11's Big Gulp to shame. I'm not real sure why anyone would want this much beer because even in January there is no way it's still cold when you get to the bottom. Come to think of it, I guess even if you get to the bottom without passing out, I doubt you care the temperature of your drink anymore. So, we each bought one to find out.

The next morning comes and surprisingly no hangover shows up for me, can't speak for the other two. After packing and checking out of the hotel, we discuss trying to leave our car somewhere that we won't have to pay long term parking or just giving in and fork up the dough. One of the biggest pains is having to pay for long term parking at the ship terminal. It's easily going to cost over $100. Sure that comes with the guarantee that it won't be towed away to some scrap yard in Louisiana, but no guarantee that it will come out unscathed. The number of door dings that happen in that place must reach somewhere close to infinity. The cars in these garages are crammed so tight that we had to unload the car of luggage and people before actually pulling into the spot. That is with every cruise terminal parking I've ever been to.

Like i said, this is my first cruise. It is not Katie's and technically not Dan's either, though his was aboard the *USS Iwo Jima* and not the fabulous *Carnival Elation*. My first look at a cruise ship was shocking. Obviously, the ships are big, and this one isn't even close to the biggest in the Carnival fleet. But dang! The colossal ship before me was so unexpected. The largest ships I had seen in my life was either a barge in the Kentucky Lake or The Tom Sawyer, a river boat that chugs up and down the Mississippi. If you ever go, however big you think the ship is going to be, it will be bigger.

Tip: when going on a cruise, unless you get an upgrade because you've reached VIP status or something, just get the cheapest option. Even if it's on the lower deck and doesn't have any windows, just get the cheaper option. You're just going to be sleeping there. The top floors don't have some secret block party at night or magical layer attached to them. The entire ship is one big party and you don't need an ocean view to have a good time.

We got to our stateroom and decided sleeping arrangements. Apparently age is not a factor in that decision, only height. Guess who the shortest of our trio is, that's right it's me. I was voted to the top bunk by my younger yet taller friends. It worked out well for me though, being on the top bunk on a massive ship in the middle of the ocean will rock you to sleep better than a back porch swing on a spring day. Other than the fear of breaking my neck or leg or face descending that ladder in the dark when I had to pee, it was five nights of some of the best sleep I'd ever had.

If you've never seen a stateroom on a cruise ship, they are quaintly little things. The interior rooms especially. They can make a college dorm seem like the honeymoon suite at The Ritz. With enough desk space for a pen, pad, one cellphone charger and maybe a bottle of water, we all had our junk situated like a game of Tetris. The bathroom is somehow smaller than you'd

THE FIRST CRUISE

expect, and don't expect much. One of the best descriptions/warnings I've ever heard for the bathroom on a cruise ship came from one of the on-board comedians. "Men, you better decide what number you've got to go before you get in there, you can't change your mind later, there is no turning around."

For those worry warts out there, who have watched *Titanic* too many times, don't fret. Cruise ships have plenty of lifeboats, rafts and life jackets for everyone. Something that you will learn in the mandatory muster station drill. Confession... For the longest time I thought it was pronounced mustard station, not muster. Hopefully I'm not alone there. Each room is stocked with plenty of charming life jackets, not as fashionable as the white ones seen on *The Titanic*, but a lovely road cone orange, complete with a whistle and blinky light. So, no worries, if you do find yourself in the middle of the ocean you won't have to take a whistle off a frozen dead body to get the rescuers attention.

Another thing included in the milk carton sized rooms are a charming set of bathrobes. Dan did a fantastic fashion show for us, ending with him lying on his bunk whipping his "high and tight" hair back stating, "Paint me like one of your French girls".

Something that you might not realize when sailing out of New Orleans is that it takes a while before you actually get to the Gulf of Mexico. When looking at the map, NOLA seems like it is right there on the edge of the ocean. However, the actual port of New Orleans is about 6 hours from the open waters of the gulf.

We were at the fancy dinner, held each night in the formal dining rooms. I say fancy because there is more than one fork and you can't wear flip flops. Katie and I decide to take a selfie. I was very close to posting it on Facebook, since we were still in the Mississippi and the land of cell service, when Dan has a panicked moment.

"DO NOT tag me in that!"

"Okay??" Katie and I just look at each other confused. Trying to figure out why he doesn't want to be seen with us??

"I didn't exactly get permission to leave the country."

Wait, What!?

Apparently, he was supposed to get permission to leave the country! Daniel did not have it! We were harboring an AWOL sailor the next five days and we only found out because of an almost Facebook update. Guess it's going to look like it's just me and Katie on this trip.

Nope, no Dan here, haven't seen him.

Later when we got home, the rule "it's easier to ask for forgiveness than permission" must have applied because we all posted so many pictures of our amazing trip. Pictures of things words can't describe enough. Beautiful beaches in Cozumel, the unworldly blue of the Caribbean Ocean, masked Luchadores wrestlers, Palm trees, amazing sunsets, and sunrises, and one of the New Wonders of the World, Chichén Itzá.

Our first port of call was in Progreso, Mexico. Dan decided we should go see some Mayan ruins while we were there. Katie and I were on the fence about visiting this place. We didn't know much about it, and it would take all day, leaving no beach time and very little shopping time. Plus, traveling that far away from port made me a bit nervous. It took two hours by bus to get there, and I didn't really know anything about it. I am so glad Dan talked us into this though.

One thing to know about doing excursions at the ports – You will have so many options. As soon as you leave the ship, you will be hounded with people offering to take you on all the adventures. From Jeep rides, beach trips, historical tours, Segway tours, scuba and snorkeling, glass bottom boats, and so much more I can't even list them all. There is the option of booking with the cruise ship itself too. That option is more expensive, but it comes with the added security of being back to the ship, guaranteed, before it leaves, or it doesn't leave without you. Being back before the ship leaves is not always a guarantee when booking with the locals, however it's less expensive and you might have more options on where to go. Something to keep in mind, should you decide to go.

This cruise, since we were barely 22, and had slim to no money, so we went with the locals and decided to risk it. When we got off the ship, we found a local with tours to Chichén Itzá, got our tickets and boarded the bus. The bus ride there was uneventful. Thankfully it was a larger charter bus complete with air conditioning, so the ride was mostly comfortable and smooth. It was a full bus, so the three of us were separated a bit, I was seated behind a very smiley Asian fella. He reminded me of my friend Roger from China, yes, Roger is his name, his American name anyway. I don't think I've ever seen Roger not smiling! Maybe it's a Asian thing?

The two-hour ride took us through Merida, the capitol of the Yucatán. Also, along the countryside through the *Reserva Estatal Geohidrologica Anillo de Cenotes*. Which according to Google Earth means 'Nature preserve in Mexico'. I'll have to take Google's word for it, my Spanish is pretty pathetic.

Maybe I'm a bit of a nerd, or have too much of my mother's DNA, but I enjoyed the drive more than I thought I would. Looking out the window checking the sights and landscape of another country was way more interesting than I thought it would be. The different vegetation and signage for businesses, how different, yet how exactly the same American fast-food places look, all were totally mesmerizing. I remember the first speed limit sign I noticed said '90' and my brain immediately thinks miles per hour instead of kilometers per hour, I thought that Mexico just threw caution to the wind when it came to traffic safety. I still think that is partly true after riding in a taxi through the city.

Designated a UNESCO world heritage site, the Mayan ruins of Chichén Itzá, is one of the "New Wonders of the World", and so worth a visit if you get the chance. The Pyramid of Kukulcan is the main attraction, but certainly not the only thing worth viewing. Temples, alters, houses, smaller pyramids, and other platforms (that are used for Lord knows what, and honestly, I'm afraid to ask) litter this site. There is even a "ball court", which was an arena like area that the Mayan people played sports in. There were massive structures all around that have no business being built by people with only hand tools. Like the pyramids of Egypt and the Great Wall, I will never understand how this could be completed without the tools and equipment we have today.

Photo opportunities are all around in this area. The giant pyramid was my favorite, we took so many pictures in front of this guy, Katie and me, Dan and me, Katie and Dan, all three of us, and the pyramid by itself. Personally I think you can't take too many pictures on vacation. What if this is your only chance to visit this place? What if you took a blurry one? What if some random dude was picking his wedgie in the background? Take all the pictures!

When our allotted time was up on the ruin grounds we had to walk the path back to the bus. Which just so happened to be right past some souvenir booths with 'authentic' Mayan calendars and masks carved from wood. I put authentic in quotes because, stupid American party of one, I have no clue what an authentic Mayan Mask would look like. However, we took their word for it, and each got one or two for ourselves and/or our family.

As we loaded up the bus, as the creatures of habit that we humans are, we all took our same seats. Not because they were assigned, and I doubt anyone would have cared, but just like on the first day of school or at church, or wherever, the first spot you sit will most likely be where you sit the remainder of your time there. Up unto this point there had been no drama, no accidents, no 'oh crap' moments.

Until now.

Luckily the problem was not our problem. Remember when I explained that booking an excursion guaranteed you'd be on the boat before it left, or it wouldn't leave. If you went through the local tour guides you took the risk of being stranded. Well, that happy go lucky Asian fella that sat in front of me on the way, never showed up to the bus for the ride back to the ship. The driver knew the passenger count was off, and we waited as long as possible, but he never showed. To this day I still wonder what happened to him. Did he hitch a ride back to the ship? Did he have to fly to wherever home was, out of Mexico? Or did he make a life for himself on the Yucatán Peninsula, being happy and smiley, maybe giving tours of the Mayan ruins? I hope it's the latter, he seemed really excited to be there.

So, I say go. I was hesitant about this excursion, but it was a once in a lifetime opportunity. Even if you have to take a "boring bus ride". Even if you are nervous about being back to your ship in time. Even if history and ancient civilizations aren't high on your list of things to see. This place should be, it's unlike anything I've ever seen before. Go anyway! How often do you get to say you've seen a 'New Wonder of the World'.

Just make sure you get to the bus on time.

The following was a note file on my phone dated January 12, 2013. It's a list of quotes and things we wanted to remember from our trip. Katie and I wrote this on our way back to Missouri, so we wouldn't forget. It is now over 10 years later so some of them I remember the context some I do not, but really wish I did. I included them anyway....

"Just make a fist when you're mad and think of me!"- Will, one of the old biker dudes we made friends with, in NOLA.

"Never make your Mom cry!!"- Cindy, one of the biker chicks we made friends with, in NOLA, also Will's wife.

"This is your cruise diiiiiii-rector Willie"- Willie Lee, the cruise director

"WHY DID YOU LET US SLEEP TILL 4PM!?!?!", included again because it was just so funny. Yelling at me while also trying to get dressed, absolute panic in Katie's voice that a whole day of vacation was wasted. I laughed till I cried. Apparently, her phone just decided to give out some random time, because even if it was still on Missouri time it would have only been an hour off.

"Turn the speaker off I'm cold"- Katie half asleep.

"We rented this boat!" Dan to some random stranger on the ship. Technically not wrong, I guess.

"What are you eating!? I've never seen one of those!" random drunk guy at lunch on the ship, we named him Broseph. Also, it was a chicken nugget.

"I have no idea what time that is." Katie, when giving her any time in military time.

"Oh my gosh, Dan is going to kill me." Me and/or Katie at least once a day.

"Would you like a blowfish?", really wish I knew what this was about.

"Loose something buddy?", not sure about this one either.

"Considering there's nothing but water outside!!" I'm not 100% on who said this, but my money is on Katie.

"We love you, Tri!" Tri was the name of our waitress at fancy dinner, she was from the Philippines, and she said her mother named her Tri because she was the third daughter. Possibly a lie but she seemed like a genuinely good person, so we are going to say it's legit.

"This chicken is on point!!" Broseph, after he found his own chicken nuggets.

Chapter 7
Memphis, TN

Next stop, Memphis, Tennessee! Home to the Beale st., BBQ, and baby Cardinals. Not to mention blues, brews and... rock'n'roll, I couldn't think of another 'b' word.

This city gets visited multiple times by my family and I. One, because it's less than four hours away and two, because I-55 runs directly through it, a major highway to the Gulf of Mexico.

Situated right on the Mississippi river, it is about 3 hours and 45 minutes from my hometown. Easy to travel to, and the short drive makes it the perfect city for a weekend getaway. Memphis probably isn't on everyone's top five for city sightseeing. It's not the most welcoming, no major attractions except maybe one or two, and the crime rate is more than some are willing to risk.

It's not NYC with the promise of designer shopping and the sign of hope for all immigrants, the Statue of Liberty. Nor is it Los Angeles, with fame and fortune around every corner. But it is special in its own way. Many blues and rock'n'roll artists made their start here. Aretha Franklin, Elvis,

Johnny Cash, Jerry Lee Lewis. It was also a major city in the civil rights movement and the heartbreaking assassination of Dr. Martin Luther King Jr. It is home to St. Jude Children's Research Hospital, a hope to sick kids and relief of financial burden for those parents.

The first thing that most likely comes to mind when someone says Memphis, however, is either Beale Street or Graceland, both of which I have visited, but you can find more if you are willing to look.

The main reason we like to travel to Memphis is to see the Memphis Redbirds, a minor league team of the St. Louis Cardinals.

St. Louis will always be baseball heaven in my opinion, win or lose Unfortunately as I write this the cardinals are well below .500 and it pains me terribly to type that. Memphis is where our baby birds learn to get their training wings off, see what I did there. As a baseball fan I highly recommend going to see the minor league games. The tickets are cheaper, the food is cheaper, the beer is cheaper, the stadiums are smaller, the atmosphere is just different. You never know when you might see the next Trout or Harper or Pujols.

One trip was made spur of the moment by my Mom and me. I had a few days off and so did she. Just so happened it was during the few days in between the end of MLB spring training season and the start of regular season. In previous years Memphis would host a preseason scrimmage. Battle of the Birds. A one game exhibition between the Memphis Redbirds and the St. Louis Cardinals. A perfect chance to get one more spring training game in, with the camaraderie of playing with brothers. No pressure to win, just another chance to have fun while playing baseball.

Mom and I had a blast, we had great seats by some stroke of luck, only a few rows up from the Cardinals dugout. We got great pictures of all our favorites from that year, Coach Willie McGee, Wacha, Waino, Yadi, and it was Goldschmidt's first year with the team, oh what high hopes we had that spring. It was a great game and a great atmosphere. I hope one day they will bring Battle of the Birds back.

What I don't hope to repeat from that trip is the flu, which I contracted at some point on that trip, my drive home I felt like death.

Nor do I ever want another speeding ticket like the one I received in the mail a few days after the trip. Not a typo, it was a speeding ticket. Not a toll fine, or a parking ticket, or even a red-light ticket. A speeding ticket. In the mail. What a wonderful way to end a fun weekend.

I ended up writing the check for this speeding ticket. Even though neither one of us was sure who was actually driving when we passed the trooper with a radar and a camera. I took the fall for it, some would be surprised that Mom didn't take the hit for it since it was her car, and moms usually do take one for the team. "Lead foot" however couldn't have another speeding ticket on her license or she would be going back to traffic school. Yes, back to traffic school. We split the bill in the end, I just wrote the check.

Stay awesome Tennessee.

I've taken many a trip to Memphis, with my bestie Heather, my sister, my momma, my momma and sister, and trips with the whole fam. Most of these trips were never more than a weekend, some just passing through. Like the time on our way to New Orleans when we somehow missed the turn to continue onto I-55 and ended up in a rather shady part of Memphis. I blame my brother-in-law. Great guy, terrible sense of direction! At least we found a Wendy's while trying to make our way back to the highway. A frosty and fries can always make an unscheduled detour seem okay.

If you are like my family and I, you probably steer clear of the chain restaurants while staying in a foreign city. I can eat at Applebee's and Pasta House at home. Give me the hole in the wall restaurants that no one has ever heard of when I'm on vacation.

One of those, we found in Memphis, sits right on Beale Street. The Rum Boogie Café. The name itself is enough to pull you in. The inside is full of guitars hanging from everywhere. Dollar bills line the walls, ceiling, and tables. I always like to look at as many of the bills to see if I recognize any of the signatures that adorn them, maybe someone I know, or maybe a celeb? You never know who could be on the famous Beale. I recommend the BLT po'boy. Not your everyday BLT, this guy comes with fried green tomatoes! It's fried, it's tangy, it's got bacon, it's delicious. I can only assume the remainder of the menu is just as good, I have blinders when it come to the Rum Boogie Café, only po'boys for me.

Another favorite lunch or dinner stop we like is Aldo's Pizza Pies. A New York-style pizza joint that sits on South Main Street on the west side of town. It can easily be walked to if staying downtown, or if you're the one in the group that hates walking everywhere, the trolly rolls right by it. We've only taken the trolly once or twice because we apparently "love" walking. Which is true for the most part, but how often do you get to ride on a trolly, unless you live in San Francisco.

All the pizza's I've tried at Aldo's were great, however when in Memphis you should obviously get the pie titled "The Memphis". It's a BBQ pizza, with BBQ sauce, cheese, pulled pork, red onion, and a giant dollop of creamy coleslaw. The first time I had this particular pie, I was with my sister, and it was the first time we had visited the city. A weekend just the two of us, no kids, no parents, no rules. We did what we wanted, when we wanted.

We were walking along main street when we found Aldo's and decided to stop for lunch. I thought she was outside her mind getting a pizza that had BBQ and coleslaw on it. Turns out I was the one in the wrong. Coleslaw on BBQ is fantastic and even better when it comes in pizza form.

A few other notable places to visit if you're ever in town, in my nonprofessional opinion anyway, The Memphis Zoo, Mud Island Park, and The

MEMPHIS, TN

Bass Pro shop. Yes, the Bass Pro is an "attraction", any small-town hillbilly will tell you the same. Take any small-town country "kid" to the city, we are finding The Bass Pro.

The Memphis Zoo, pretty self-explanatory. Animals; Lions and tigers and bears, Oh My! And lots of walking. The entrance and the zoo itself has a great Egyptian theme. Paying tribute to Memphis, Egypt, the former capital of Lower Egypt. The zoo itself is over 100 years old, old but not quite in the same ballpark as actual Egypt, and it hosts thousands of animals. So, if an animal lover or you want to feel like a kid for an afternoon, the zoo, in Memphis or anywhere really, should always be on the list.

Mud Island was an accidental find, but so fun and bonus - it's free! It sits in the Mississippi river, technically a peninsula and not an island, although a good flood probably makes the name very literal. It's not far from downtown and right near the Memphis Welcome Center. Mud Island has a museum that is at a cost, but the rivers eye view of the Memphis skyline and the scale model of the Mississippi river are free, and so much fun to explore.

Now, travel with me to Bass Pro. This is not some run of the mill Bass Pro, sitting in some strip mall that's made to look like a giant log cabin. This Bass Pro Shop is sitting inside of the 32-story steel Pyramid, right on the Mississippi river.

Who doesn't love a trip to The Bass Pro, outdoorsman or not! Where else can someone get a new ATV, green apple licorice (the king of all licorice), camping gear, and a new 4th of July tee shirt every summer? Bass Pro that's where! Not only does this location have all your outdoor needs, but it also host a bowling alley, archery range, bar and grill, and Americas tallest freestanding elevator, oh and you can even stay the night at the Big Cypress Lodge inside the store.

If not an outdoorsy person and you have no desire to see the probably 37 varieties of camo they have, you should at least take the elevator to the top of the pyramid. There is a beautiful observation deck at the top, with incredible views of Memphis.

And if you feel like being a bit mischievous, like myself, don't tell the one person in the group that is afraid of heights that the floor is see through on the observation deck. Boy was my sister mad at me! She gasped and jumped back so fast you would have thought there was a rattlesnake on the deck. She did grab my arm and pull me back with her, saving me from my nonexistent 300ft freefall on to Bass Pro Dr. before she started yelling. Safety over scolding. It took about 15 mins or so before she could step out on the deck without her legs shaking but after that we got some great views of a Memphis sunset from the top. Plus, she gained a new skill of almost overcoming heights, something she would need on later trips.

Now, the moment you've been waiting for.

A core memory for me and one of the moments I was 115% sure my mother was going to jail, was during a trip to Memphis. This was a weekend trip with my momma and my sister and me, no kids, but now I know that we really could've used their supervision.

We went on this trip to do the typical touristy things. Walk Beale Street, eat BBQ, and of course, visit the home of the King of Rock 'n Roll, Graceland. Unless you were born yesterday, you know who I am talking about. Elvis Presley. My Mom was and is an Elvis fan, having grown up in the '60s and '70s. She will be the first to say that it was her older sister, Cindy, who was obsessed with Elvis. What teenage girl wasn't?

My sister also grew up in the '70s (I'm going to receive a death stare when she finds out I've told y'all this). However she was only 2 when he died in 1977, so, yes probably a fan but not as much as the generation before her. I like most of his songs and of course that sexy leg shake he does, I guess that probably makes me a fan as well. My fandom comes mostly by association, from my Mom listening to Elvis in the car, my dad singing Elvis at random, and my big brother Josh being one small step from Uncle Jesse in *Full House*. He can even do the whole lip curl, leg shake, while giving us the *"Uh-huh"*.

On this particular trip we did a tour that included Graceland and Sun Studio. Transportation included from one to the other from downtown Memphis. So being the adventurers we are, we left the Jeep parked at the hotel and walked to our starting point of the tour, Sun Studios, on the corner of Union and Marshall. Well, that walk should have been the first clue that this trip was going to be interesting.

The walk took far longer than we anticipated through streets that didn't exactly scream "3 women totally safe here". Mom didn't seem too concerned with the neighborhood, but that's just who she is, she doesn't worry or panic about much, must be a nurse thing.

Sun studios is worth a visit when in Memphis. If you don't have enough time to do the whole big thing with Graceland, I recommend Sun Studios. So many greats have recorded in that very building, Elvis, Johnny Cash, and Jerry Lee Lewis.

We did our walk around through Sun Studios. We pretended we were rock n' roll stars while touring the recording booth. I even grabbed the 1950s era microphone and acted like I was belting out the best notes anyone had ever heard this side of the Mississippi. Note I said I "acted" like I'm singing because had I really belted it out, the other patrons of Sun Studios that day would have sued for ear damage.

We enjoyed our time at Sun Studio, but now it's time to board the small shuttle bus with the other 20 or so visitors that day, and take the 15-minute drive to 3734 Elvis Presley Boulevard. We are dropped off at the entrance to the line to enter the grounds. After 15 -20 minutes of zig zagging through roped off lines, we finally near the start of our tour of the King of Rock n' Roll's home.

This is where I witness my mother turn white as a sheet and break out in a cold sweat.

With more panic than I have ever seen on her face, she is looking at me and Lisa wondering what to do next. Still unsure the cause of panic, we look to her then look to each other. Mom has her purse clutched so tight in her hands; I'm turning around looking for potential robbers.

Mom, trying not to show the entire place her worry and bring attention to us, purse still in a death grip, motions toward the front of the line. It's then that we notice the security guard, "wanding" people with a metal detector and searching purses.

Lisa and I look toward the guard, then at each other, then to Mom. It is at that moment she gets really close, so that only we can hear her speak.

"I have a gun in my purse."

Insert stomach drop.

My Mom is going to jail. Not only is she going to jail, but she's also going to jail in another state. We don't even have a car!

"Yes, excuse me, Mr. Graceland bus driver sir? Can you take me back to my car, I have to go get my mother out of Memphis jail for illegally taking a concealed unauthorized weapon into a public place."

I am as freaked out as my mother, and she is the one I look to when I am freaked out. So, now I'm freaked out, and my mother is freaked out, and my sister had to be freaking out and now I don't know what to do with my freak out because they are freaked out.

My sister was very quiet. Either she was also internally freaking out about how to get Mom out of Memphis jail, or hopefully... trying to figure out a way to get us out of this particular situation.

Our time is up, we are next to go in. I have no idea what to do.

Now, this could be seen as either the luckiest day, or the unluckiest day. No one went to jail. Not a ticket. Not a warning. Nothing. Nada.

Mr. Security guard waved his little metal detector around us, and got out his little purse poker stick, that looks like one half a pack of chopsticks, and went through Lisa's purse, then my purse, and finally Mom's arsenal, I mean purse.

"All set. Enjoy Graceland." He says very happily. Mom takes her purse back, udders an inaudible "Thank you.". None of us breathe until we walk in.

We couldn't believe it! He completely missed it!?

We are now packing heat in Graceland!

Now that we can breathe, we do enjoy Graceland! We walk the grounds of his estate. We visit Elvis' gravesite, where he is laid to rest between his father and grandmother. We opted for the audio tour, which included an MP3 player that will give you facts and info about wherever you are in the house or on the grounds. The house is unlike anything I've ever seen. So unique and so Elvis. White carpets, gold trim, and just Elvis like. I would expect nothing less from the King of Rock n' Roll. My favorite room was probably not even considered a room, but it was where his white grand piano sat in a room off of a room. I wondered how many times he sat at that piano, telling the ivories his problems, or writing the next biggest hit, or singing to his family on Christmas morning. Graceland is really something today but imagine what it was like in its heydays.

Graceland has a bit of mystery too it as well, as if it wasn't interesting enough. While on our tour, we noticed the second floor is closed off. It is said to be so "out of respect for the family". Which is totally understandable, personally it seems pretty morbid to want to see the room that Elvis, died in and no family should have that displayed for the whole world to see either. However, there are the select few that believe Elvis never really died that August day in 1977. So, could it be that there is no 'death room', maybe there was no death that day, maybe Elvis is really living upstairs this whole time, and all his fans have no idea how close they could be to him.

Just a little conspiracy theory for all of you.

The more I think back on that trip to Graceland, there is one thing I can't help but wonder. No, I am not one of the few who believe Elvis is still alive, I don't actually think he is living upstairs in his mansion or a beach in Hawaii.

I wonder, how many others ended up bringing a gun in their purse that day and also almost had a heart attack while waiting in line. How did that security guard miss it? Did my mother not seem like much of a threat? Did he really not see or feel it in there, even with his very sophisticated security tool, his leftover chopsticks from the hibachi grill.

We may never know.

Chapter 8
The Bahamas

In 2016 we, as a family, decided to start a great tradition. One that unfortunately got put on hold due to the COVID outbreak of 2020. Hopefully soon we can restart this wonderful Christmas tradition, so that I won't have to try to find actual Christmas presents anymore.

It started with a small conversation with my sister, at church even, (we are not perfect listeners sometimes) I can still remember the look on her face when I had the idea. I knew my Mom had been wanting to go on a big family vacation, like when we went to Florida or Vegas, but because life is crazy, we hadn't done so in a long time. I also had been wanting to go on another cruise, my first one was such a blast, and I wanted my family to experience this as well.

One day at church somewhere between the singing and the sermon I said to Lisa "Let's go on a cruise instead of buy Christmas presents for each other."

She looked at me, furrowed brow, very quizzical in thought like I just had the most brilliant idea I've ever had. To be fair, she gives me that look a lot, everyone does, I have a lot of great ideas.

It snowballed from there, for the next 4 years that's what we, as a family, did for Christmas. We went on some cruise, somewhere. Until COVID hit we cruised, and even after COVID we still managed a family Christmas trip to Wisconsin.

Other than myself, one niece and my brother-in-law, the remainder of the family would be first time cruisers. After a long discussion with Mom, a lot of planning, and being very sneaky, the date was set. Christmas present for 2015 would be a cruise to The Bahamas in January of 2016.

Now, don't you worry, the Christmas tree was not completely bare that year. It was for the majority of December, which was pretty concerning to a couple of 10- and 11-year-olds.

"Mom! Christmas is next week!"

"Yeah?" unconcerned.

"There aren't any presents under the tree??"

"Well, yeah, Santa hasn't come yet."

"Mother."

This was a conversation between Lisa and my niece Emily. "Mother" was accompanied by the ever-popular eye roll teenagers are so gifted at. The whole cruise for Christmas was a complete surprise to the girls, as per their concern over no presents under the tree. Brenden was in on the little secret, so that he could prepare his basketball coach he would be missing a few games.

A few school days would also have to be missed for this trip. Some may recoil at the thought of missing school "just for a vacation". To each their own, but the things kids, and adults as well, can learn from traveling the world will forever outrank the classroom. So much can be learned with travel. History, geography, how to interact with people of a different culture, different traditions around the world, and in the case of most of our vacations, how to think on your feet and navigate the "wrench" in the plan.

Christmas arrives and to the girls' relief, "Santa" showed up and there were presents under the tree. Not a lot, mind you, but enough to make this surprise very fun. Emily and Issy were opening their presents with a bit of confusion. These were not typical gifts from their parents.

Tanks and shorts in December?
Crazy sunglasses?
What do we need sunscreen for, it's 30° outside?
What on earth is.... Dimenhydrinate???

After a few minutes of confused looks, Lisa finally starts asking them how they like their gifts. Being the good kids they were, they did not come right out and say "they are super weird" but it was written all over their faces.

"Well, maybe these gifts are a clue to your actual gift." She told them. Something that definitely caught their attention. "Now you have to guess what it is!"

You could see their minds racing. Looking at each clue, sunglasses, sunscreen, summer clothes. At a point you could see the realization in their eyes, they were afraid to say it out loud, in case they were wrong.

"Are we... going on a trip?" Full hesitation in Issy's voice as she asked it.

When no denial came from Lisa, Mom, me or Doug (Lisa's husband), Emily asked with slightly more confidence, yet still afraid of the rug being pulled out from under her, "Somewhere warm, maybe?"

"Can you guess where?" Lisa asked.

Excitement growing, they started naming off every possible driving destination from Missouri. Florida being their best guess.

"Nope, look at the last clue."

"Dimenhydrinate? We don't even know what that is!"

"What does the box say?"

After frantic searching, looking for the answer to the million-dollar question, someone finally tells them it's to treat motion sickness.

"Oh! Oh! I know!! Are we going on a cruise?" chimes in Issy ecstatic!

Shocked excitement jolts out of the both of them when Lisa nods, telling them we will be going on a 5-day cruise to the Bahamas the first week of January.

"WAIT! For real? Like you're being for real right now??"

The look on their faces was pure gold. It was by far the most fun we've had in giving them a Christmas present.

Our cruise left out of Charleston, South Carolina. A long drive for us but a scenic drive at least. It's about fourteen-hour drive from my home in Missouri, crossing through Illinois, Kentucky, Tennessee, North Carolina, and finally South Carolina. Conveniently for my mother, I-24 passes right near her home in Kentucky, so we just picked her up along the way. This road trip was way more scenic than the trip to New Orleans. Crossing the Appalachian Mountain range, we got beautiful views going up and down and around the Great Smoky Mountains, though many National Forests and even through a few tunnels. Even though a longer drive, the views made it more enjoyable.

We gave ourselves one extra day in Charleston. Just to check things out and to make sure we had plenty of time to get there. No fun in rushing. "I don't like to be rushed!" is my mother's motto.

Charleston has a beautiful historic downtown. Full of old buildings from 200 plus years ago, from old brickwork to cobblestone alleyways, you can just tell there is so much history here. Some of my favorites were the multicolored buildings. The pastel colors of pink, blue, and yellow, a coastal palate coating each building, complete with palms lining the streets.

I would love to go back to check out more of downtown, I'm certain there are some pretty great hidden treasures throughout Charleston.

My family and I are kind of National Park nerds. We love a good Nat. Park. Big ones, small ones, ones we've already been to, National Parks, National Monuments, Historical Landmarks, National Forests, whatever. Charleston has a great amount of all of those, so we gave ourselves some time to visit at least one.

We chose to visit Fort Sumter National Monument. Home of the first shots of the Civil War. Fort Sumter sits on an island right at the entrance to the Charleston Harbor. It can only be accessed by boat, or I guess someone braver than me could swim to it but that's probably frowned upon.

Two unexpected things happened on our 30-minute ferry ride to the island. One, we got to see some dolphins swimming in the harbor, raising their bodies out of the water just enough for a fresh breath and even a few that did a little jump for us. This was by far, a way more successful dolphin viewing trip than our last, not once did I think we were going to die on this boat trip, and that wasn't even why we were here! It was just a bonus!

Secondly, out of left field Emily shouts when she first notices the dolphins "I see dorsal fins!! I see dorsal fins!!"

What!?!

Our whole team looked at her as if she was speaking a different language. We all knew what a dorsal fin was, yes, but that's not something that comes across our everyday vocabulary in small town Missouri, and it is definitely not something we expected out of my eleven-year-old niece.

"You see what??" one of us asked in bewilderment.

"A dorsal fin! Look!!" annoyance in her voice like we were a bunch of idiots. "It's the fin on the back of a dolphin, and other ocean animals." We were getting schooled in science from a 6th grader.

Us. With the college degrees. IN SCIENCE!

She is a smart kid, must take after her aunt!

"How on earth do you know what a dorsal fin is?"

"Mom, I go to school. And I'm gonna be a marine psychologist when I grow up."

Ahh, so close kid. Yep, definitely takes after her aunt.

"It's biologist, idiot!" Brothers, always keeping you humble.

We had great fun with that the remainder of the trip. Dorsal fins and marine psychology.

The Fort is a great visit if you are ever in Charleston. Full of history. Lots of war relics from bunkers and black cannons to rust colored brick ruins of the Fort itself. And of course, Old Glory raised high for everyone around to see. Plus, you get great views of the Charleston harbor and Atlantic Ocean. It's a great place to walk around and imagine what went on there, how many lives were changed at that small island. Some for better, some for worse. Worth a visit if you have time.

This cruise was a five-day voyage to the Bahamas, stopping at Freeport and the capitol of The Bahamas, Nassau on the *Carnival Fantasy*. It was my sister who happen to point out how "spicy" the Carnival fleet sounds. Fantasy, Elation, Dream. Ooo lala. Insert flashy eyebrows. *The Fantasy* has since been decommissioned, and the newer ships in the fleet aren't quite so scandalously named. Happier names like *Mardi Gras* and *Jubilee*, not something that belongs in a dirty romance novel.

The town of Freeport was our first stop, it's located on Grand Bahama Island. As I've mentioned earlier about excursions, we chose not to book though the ship and just found some locals offering tours. We even went a step further and told a taxi driver "take us to a place we can snorkel". This was the one thing I had been looking forward to the most. A real snorkeling excursion.

THE BAHAMAS

The taxi driver took us out of town to a little "resort" in a quieter area of the island. Driving throughout other countries will always be interesting to me. It's interesting to see how the rest of the world lives, travels, and goes about their everyday. It is something that has always fascinated me.

The place the taxi driver chose did not disappoint. He wasn't exaggerating when he said a quieter area of the island. No shops, no other resorts, no other buildings either. Our "resort" was even just a speckle of a few small buildings complete with the thatched roofs. There were only about 15 other people at the "resort" as well. We had a great time at that place. I would love to recommend it to you all but all I know is tell the third taxi driver in line at the port that you want to snorkel at a private beach. Sorry I'm not more helpful there.

We swam, we snorkeled, I got great pictures with my Gopro of a cute little blue and yellow fish that was my favorite, (a Blue-Headed Wrasse if you want to know), we built sandcastles, walked along the beach, and the resort had a competition of egg toss for a prize. Brenden and I teamed up for the little battle and we actually won! Somehow an awkward teenager and this girl that hasn't played ball in a while managed to gently toss the egg without it breaking at the farthest distance. Not surprising at all, our prize was a bottle of rum. I was a little surprised they let the 15-year-old have it, his mother didn't find it quite as amusing as I did. No worries though. I promised him and Lisa, I would save it for when he turns 21 and we will enjoy the winnings together. Legally.

Next stop was the capitol of The Bahamas, Nassau. A bustling city, with lots of resorts, lots of cruise ships and lots, and lots of tourists.

We decided the beach is where we wanted to spend the day again. Once again, we found a friendly taxi driver with a vehicle large enough for all 7 of us and told him we'd like to go to the beach. He said "sure hop in", but he could only take us to the free public beach, all private beaches would be full without a reservation. No problem, a public beach sounds fine. Yeah, remember when I said lots and lots of tourists? Well, I am certain that almost all of those lots and lots were at this particular beach.

The beach was beautiful at least, white sand, turquoise waters, cloudless sky, what should be a textbook perfect beach day. Had it not been for a few minor hiccups it would have been perfect. We had to set our towels up on the back-40 of this beach, nowhere near the water. Apparently, we were the last to arrive. We even got lucky enough to be stationed right next to a group of college kids. Blasting rap music in a foreign language. Before you get in a tizzy, I do not have a problem with music in a language other than English, I have multiple songs in my music library in other languages. I do however, dislike when people play music in places it's not necessary. i.e. the beach.

Listening to the ocean waves is one of the most relaxing and tranquil sounds our world has to offer. Why would you not want to listen to it? Furthermore, why would you force the crowd around you to do the same. That includes parks, lakes, rivers, and hiking trails.

Okay. Rant over.

Another small glitch in the perfect beach day was the ocean itself. Absolutely breathtakingly beautiful, with its light turquoise waters shimmering like Edward Cullen in the sun. It was so pretty. It was not however, easy to swim in. I think I'm still pulling sand out my ears. The waves were so rough if you didn't make it through the break or weren't prepared for the wave coming at you, you were getting tossed on your hind end. When you did get tossed, good luck getting back up because the next wave was coming at you post haste and the ocean doesn't allow time-outs.

The day wasn't a complete failure though. Brenden convinced me and Lisa to go parasailing, I tried to get Mom to go also but she declined the invite stating, "I've already been parasailing before". *Mom, it's the Caribbean, you went parasailing in Missouri, that's not exactly the same thing.* No go, she stayed back with the nieces and brother-in-law to enjoy the rough waves and Italian rap music.

The fellas that took us on our tour were great. Funny and friendly, and they put us at ease if we had any questions. There was one question that Lisa needed answered before she would consent to getting strapped in and eventually "dipped" in the water while attached to her parasail.

"Uhh... Are there any sharks out here?"

With a flirtatious chuckle the guide pointed back to himself with a thumb and in that wonderful Caribbean accent goes "I'm dee only shaawk, in dee's watas!"

Well... Ok then.

One of the best conversations I've ever overheard was in Nassau. While souvenir shopping along the port a stranger, presumably from the Bahamas from his accent. Random stranger guy walks up to The Doug "Hey man! Want some weed?" he says very friendly like.

Small chuckle "Nah man, I'm on the wagon." Which I want to point out the B.I.L was not on any wagon for drugs or otherwise. He does not have an addiction problem, he just figured that was a good response to get this dealer to go away. Well, he was wrong.

"Oh ok.... Want some heroin then??"

"What the hell do you think being on the wagon means? No, I don't want anything you got brother!"

I have enjoyed every cruise I've been on. I'm here for a good time, all the time. I will have to say this was the worst cruise of them all. Not the actual ship, or the ports of call. But the actual cruising. Sailing the Atlantic is way rougher than it is in the Gulf of Mexico. Something my Navy pal Dan pointed out to us after we got back, that yes, the Atlantic is brutal!

I'm not much of a motion sickness person. Roads have to be really curvy for me to get car sick, or just any road when my brother-in-law is driving, but as long as I'm shotgun, motion sickness never usually bothers me. That is not the case with some of our group. The Atlantic took full advantage of that!

I stated how rough the waters were at the public beach in Nassau. That was nothing compared to the trip to and from the islands though the Atlantic. The seas got rough, and the boat got to rocking. Motion sickness struck. Mom, Lisa, and Emily were all looking very green. Multiple trips to the gift shop on board for Dramamine and calls to room service for green apples, a helpful tip we learned from a neighboring table at dinner, green apples apparently help with nausea. Vomit bags were posted around every corner. It wasn't just our team feeling the effects. Someone in the group actually ended up purging eggs and toast all over the breakfast table one morning.

The rocking and see-sawing of the ship finally got to my sister, and she yelled at anyone that would listen...

"I WILL GIVE YOU EVERY DOLLAR IN MY BANK ACCOUNT TO GET ME A HELICOPTER OFF OF THIS BOAT!!"

Needless to say, that didn't happen. We did make it back to Charleston safe and sound with only the one instance of the vomitus. We were slightly delayed in getting off the ship, though, waiting for the Coast Guard and the DEA to remove the guy about ten staterooms down in handcuffs escorted by a very handsome looking German Shepard dog.

I guess he wasn't "on the wagon".

Chapter 9
Chicago, IL

There is a certain song that is played and sung at Wrigley Field. I'd give you a dose of it, but I can't bring myself to type it, the song makes me nauseous. Let's just say it involves the Cubs winning. Gross.

I hate this song.

The summer of 2016 we, Lisa and I, decided to take another one of our no kids, no parents trips. We chose Chicago for a few reasons. It's close, it can be reached from St. Louis via an Amtrak train, it has a lot to offer, and we've never been before. The main reason though was getting to see the St. Louis Cardinals, yay, play the Chicago Cubs, boooo.

What an absolute convenience Amtrak is. Not just for weekend trip destinations, but also for getting the niece and nephew home from college. Both chose to attend college on the other side of the state. Brenden at MWSU was able to catch a train in Kansas City for trips home. Emily is currently attending UCM, and the train stops a mere three minutes from her dorm.

Amtrak has two stops for us to choose from in the St. Louis area, one in Kirkwood, Missouri, where both the college kids travel to. And one in Downtown St. Louis, where we will be boarding for our trip to Chicago.

The train ride on the Lincoln Service doesn't save you anytime, unless you drive like my mother. The trip by train is around 5-hours give or take a few minutes. The trip via car is exactly 5 hours and 12 minutes from my address, per the Google. Once again, if you drive like my mother, then you could probably make it in 4.5 hours. That's between you, God, and your insurance though.

Another convenience of taking the train is... no car. You are probably thinking "yeah, duh". I don't just mean driving. You don't have to find parking at the hotel, you don't have to find parking at the places you visit and yeah, you also don't have to drive in city traffic. Something this girl gets to do all the time since I somehow was the designated city driver anywhere we went at 16. Anyway, the parking fees you will save alone, will cover the cost of your train ticket.

Chicago is a great place for exploring. You can walk almost everywhere, if not a fan of the walk, there are other options, water taxis, regular taxis, and the L-train or subway, whatever you want to call it. If you're really adventurous rent a scooter! A little nerve racking at first but nothing like speeding down the sidewalk and city streets, wind in your hair, and lovely sounds of traffic honking and pedestrians yelling as you nearly clip them blowing past them. Ahh bliss.

We walked.

Everywhere.

We stayed on Michigan Avenue, and no we don't make doctor money, but we did splurge a little. So, we were situated well within walking distance to so many places. Millennium Park, Navy Pier, Lake Michigan, North Island Park, Museum Campus, Buckingham Palace, and of course Michigan

Avenue Shopping district. Seriously there are so many places to check out on this one strip of the city.

We spent an entire day walking around, checking out the sights. Navy Pier was a must of course. I wasn't overly impressed, maybe I didn't spend enough time there or possibly because someone wouldn't let us get on the Ferris Wheel. Apparently, we haven't completely gotten over the fear of heights since Memphis. It was fun to walk around the massive pier getting to see Lake Michigan in all its glory.

We had gotten our first views of Lake Michigan from our walk along the Adler Planetarium Skyline Walk. Adler Planetarium sits lake front near Northerly Island Park and has a lengthy walking path right on Lake Michigan. It was here that I realized how massive lakes could be. I have seen Table Rock Lake and Lake of the Ozarks. I've swam and water skied in Kentucky and Barkley Lakes. While all vast and brilliant bodies of water, from the dark almost black waters and the viewable shorelines on each side, you never once question it's a lake.

Lake Michigan, had me guessing. Its brilliant blue, almost turquoise, waters will make you wonder if you took a wrong turn and teleported by accident to the Caribbean. The absolute freezing temperature from the overspray of waves crashing into the walkway, however, will bring you back to reality.

We went over to Millennium Park to see the famous Bean. A giant statue, you guessed it, in the shape of a bean. Its mirror coated exterior attracts people and tourist from all over the city. Bonus it's free. We are big fans of the free adventure in case you haven't noticed. Free attractions are nothing to knock. All kinds of fun can be had simply walking and exploring. Giant Bean statue? Let's get a selfie. Find an art garden of giant legs? Let's stick our heads between the legs like little kids. See a bunch of food trucks and people in one place, go check it out! You might accidently find yourself watching a skateboarding competition. Yeah, we did all those in Chicago. Accidental adventures are on another level.

Adventurers we are, so we found the opportunity to do just that, even in the big city. This wasn't free, but worth every penny to me. While walking along the Chicago River one afternoon we noticed some kayakers lazily paddling down the river. *"Well, we love to kayak!"* we thought while eating deep dish pizza that night at Giordano's, a Chicago must by the way. So, we found a company to kayak the Chicago River with.

What an adventure it was. It was very unlike the rivers at home. The Big River with at max a class 1 rapid, the Current River with its beautiful cool spring fed waters, or the St. Francois River with its racing waters perfect for whitewater competitions. No rapids, no flipping the kayaks, no disturbing the fisherman on the banks, the paddle down the Chicago was calm and relaxing, peaceful even. A different kayaking adventure than we were accustomed to.

The view of Chicago from the river is incredible. Buildings that tower over you while walking along the streets are magnified tenfold from the blueish gray waters of the Chicago River. The trip takes you upriver away from Lake Michigan. Past the amazing glass covered modern Trump Tower, complete with the more liberal set of tourists giving it the finger from every street corner, ahh the beauty of America. We even paddled down toward the more historical and gothic buildings like the 35 E Wacker Building, The London House, and The Wrigley Building. If a chocolate lover you must go in The Wrigley, not to be confused with Wrigley Field, that's a bit farther away, but the Wrigley building hosts the Ghirardelli Chocolate Shop, with all the flavors and then some. ALL OF THE FLAVORS!

There is a massive amount of water traffic in the Chicago River. Large tourist boats taking people down the river and out toward the lake, water taxies, smaller private vessels, barges hauling various products to a myriad of places, and of course the common kayak. There is also a large amount of trash in the Chicago River. Which does cause a bit of similarity between it and the Big River from back home. Random soda bottles, candy wrappers, food containers, and other typical trash. The not so typical items found on our voyage around Chicago, a ball cap, a whole dang watermelon, and most disgustingly, a used condom.

Eww. That's it. Paddle's over.

Two of the best places I have ever eaten, were in Chicago. They also were found by accident while just walking around the city.

One morning we needed coffee, and I needed food. Lisa is not much of a breakfast person, so I basically had to beg her to let us go to an actual breakfast place for coffee and breakfast. She gave in this day and boy are we both glad she did. Because a few blocks from our hotel we found a place called YOLK.

BEST. BREAKFAST. EVER.

Signature coffee, comfort and unique foods, pancake of the month and not ridiculously priced for downtown. Plus, the atmosphere is "a vibe" as the kids say. Yolk has the diner feel to it, it's bright and shiny and happy.

My personal favorite is the El Torero Scrambler. Eggs, chorizo, avocado, pepper jack, salsa, enough spice to make your guts hurt, but oh so good. The frittatas and the pancakes are also good. Highly recommend YOLK. We have made it a staple on our trips to Chicago. The next trips we took to the Windy City, every morning was spent at Yolk. We've even gone as far as looking to see if there is a Yolk nearby on every trip we've taken, no matter where we go.

The other accidental find was on our walk back to the hotel after taking a Wendella boat tour of the Chicago River and Lake Michigan.

Side story, take a boat tour of the lake. There are many companies to choose from offering all types of cruises, find one that interests you and try it. We choose Wendella because I knew a friend of mine from high school worked for Wendella, booking through them gave me a chance to catch up with her while waiting for our tour to start. Our cruise didn't go exactly according to plan. We picked the firework lake cruise, and it poured down rain for hours. Even though the rain ceased by the time we got out on the lake, the fog and clouds canceled the firework portion.

The cruise down the river and out to the lake was well worth it anyway. The Chicago Skyline lit up with the low cloud ceiling. It felt like every building had its own hue of color that glowed among the fog. It made for some awesome pictures. So don't get discouraged if it "rains on your parade" so to say, sometimes great things can come from the deviation.

Anyway, back to the restaurant. We were walking back to the hotel after our tour and decided to find something to eat. That decision couldn't have come at a better time either. Whilst waiting our turn at the crosswalk a guy dressed as the devil, walked right up beside us waiting for the same pedestrian signal we were. Complete with an ugly mug of a face, horns and goatee. Wearing a wind breaker of course, it is Chicago after all.

I know city people are eccentric but walking down the street with Satan, that was a little much for us. We found Pizano's Pizza and Pasta at the perfect moment. Best meatball sub I've ever had in my life. Heavenly even.

I have been a Cardinal fan my entire life. I don't remember not loving the Cardinals, even when they absolutely sucked. I love Cardinal baseball. I have played baseball or softball every summer or fall since I was five until well in my twenties. Every year whatever position I played, the corresponding player for the St. Louis Cardinals that year, was my favorite player. Outfield for me, Jim Edmonds for the Cardinals. Second base for me, Fernando Vina for the Cardinals, first base for Me, Albert Pujols for the

Cardinals. Picking my favorite player has evolved some since little league. Their talent and good looks played a factor in my choice. Every year, as soon as The Super Bowl party wraps up, I have my eyes set on news from spring training.

I tell you all of this because one of my bucket list items was seeing the St. Louis Cardinals play at one of the most historical stadiums. Wrigley Field.

Wrigley Field is located north of downtown Chicago and it's only a short L-Train ride away. It is the second oldest stadium in the United States and is full of baseball nostalgia.

Busch Stadium II and Busch Stadium III were the only MLB stadiums I had been to, so I wasn't sure what to expect for Wrigley. It is notably smaller than either of those structures but that only adds to it's greatness. This will be the one and only time I use the word great with anything associated with the Cubs. The stadium really is amazing though. The atmosphere, the classic ivy-covered outfield wall, the retro manual scoreboard, a sea of Cardinal red and Cubbie blue from so many fans of both teams, it's baseball in its element.

I have gotten to visit The Friendly Confines twice.

This trip with my sister was our first visit. We got tickets for the daytime game, North Chicago is not known for its safety, and for two young women in an unfamiliar city, a night game just didn't sound smart. No bother to us though, yes it was hot, yes it was humid, but that is the joy of baseball! Sweat dripping in places you don't want to talk about, legs sticking to your plastic chair, feeling like you're trying to breath underwater the air is so thick, that is baseball season in its glory.

We got decent seats, lower level under the shade of the second deck. Like one does at the airport, we made sure our seats existed before checking out the stadium and concessions, of course opting for the Chicago Dog. We had arrived early enough to catch the tail end of batting practice, so we made our way down to the first row of seats that are only separated from the field by the knee-high barrier. Crowd of kids, and adults lined the area, holding out baseballs and caps, hoping for just one player signature. I didn't have anything to get autographed, but I was totally content with the close-up pictures of the warmup tosses, batting practice, and of course the stretching.

As we stood watching the pregame shenanigans, we were near a reporter for the St. Louis Cardinals. He is a very well-known reporter if you watch Fox Sports Midwest (now Bally sports) for the games. Jim "the Cat" Hayes. We watched him give his pregame information to the camera, talking about the games pitching matchup and starting line ups. When he finished up and the camera was off, on a whim I blurted out "Jimmy the Cat!! Can we get a picture??" To my surprise he obliged let us get all the selfies we wanted and said to enjoy the game!

Cardinal baseball, Wrigley Field, sun shining, a selfie with Jimmy "the Cat", this was going to be a good day win or lose.

It was a great day!! The Cards slugged out a 7-2 win over those Cubbies to complete the three-game sweep! Checking off Wrigley Field couldn't have gone better.

A year later we decided Wrigley Field was a definite do over. It went so well the first time *let's take Mom* we thought! She is the one who introduced us to Cardinal baseball in the first place.

Most people assume if a person loves baseball or a certain sports team, that love was passed down from the male side of the family. The dad, or grandpa, or maybe a brother. Not us. Not that my father, grandpa, or brother doesn't like the Cardinals, it's hard to live in the region we do and not love Cardinal baseball. However, our love of baseball came from our mother, who got it from her mother. It's a love that goes deep in the Brewen women. Even at 91, with dementia so bad she couldn't remember my name, my grandmother could tell me with pride and excitement how much she loved baseball.

"Ooo now baseball... that's my sport!" she would say.

So, the fall of 2017 we decided to take Mom to Chicago for an early birthday get away, and so that she could check Wrigley off her bucket list as well.

We took the train from downtown St. Louis to Union Station Chicago. Got our customary "Chicago Dogs" as soon as we exited the train.

On our way to the hotel, I decided to start the argument of who is sleeping next to whom. A discussion every family has when traveling, who has to bunk together. I argued that since I went through all the trouble of booking the room, getting the train tickets, and the game tickets, I should be rewarded with my own bed, and Mom and Lisa should have to bunk together, plus they both snore so they should enjoy each other's company. Lisa argued that she is the tallest of the three, she is near 6' and I'm a measly 5'2" (5'3 with my shoes on), she therefore needs more leg room, so she needed her own bed. Mom of course, used the Mom card, and said she gets her own bed because well, she's the Mom.

The entire cab ride from Union Station to The Congress Plaza, and while checking us in, we were still discussing "arguing" the sleeping arrangements. Unbeknownst to the other two I had actually booked us a room with three beds. The look on their faces was priceless when we walked in the room and we each had our own bed. Starting family arguments for no reason is great entertainment sometimes.

We took Mom to all our favorites from our first visit. The Bean, Navy Pier, which I still did not get to ride on the Ferris Wheel in case you were wondering, kayaking the river, and a tour boat cruise on Lake Michigan. And of course, breakfast at Yolk.

The weekend was great. Until.

The game.

Not that we didn't have fun, baseball is always fun. Always. But after a go-ahead Jason Heyward single in the 7th inning and no more runs from the Birds, things turned terrible.

Before the last out is made, the crowd starts singing. Louder and louder they get, filling the entire stadium with that horrible song after the last out, and the white flag with a large blue W is raised. Cubs win.

I truly do hate that song.

Chapter 10
Wisconsin Dells, WI

We have been on many, many family vacations. All over the country and beyond. None of those destinations screamed "family friendly" like Wisconsin Dells.

The Dells is a little under 7 hours from my hometown. Passing though Missouri, Illinois, and Wisconsin, it is a rather boring drive, looking at mainly corn fields and other corn fields, but it is a better drive than through the nothingness of Mississippi. Only going in or around two major cities, St. Louis and Madison, it makes for a pretty easy destination to get to, and it has a lot to offer.

Lakes, rivers, tourist attractions, amusement parks, water parks, zoos, natural areas, you name it, the Dells have it. The specialty of the Wisconsin Dells is its waterparks. It's even nicknamed "The Waterpark Capitol of the World" due to its 20 or more indoor and outdoor waterparks.

When we go, we have always stayed at *Christmas Mountain Village,* but don't be fooled by the name, it isn't some secret "North Pole" in the Midwest. It is part of the Bluegreen Vacations, which is why we stay here,

Lisa and her husband are a part of Bluegreen Vacations. That is what allows us to go on a lot of our trips. Christmas Mountain Village is perfect, it's secluded, it is outside of town, away from all the noise and crowds, but not so far away from the fun and necessities.

The resort itself offers enough for the family that you wouldn't have to go into town if you didn't want to. It has golf, tennis, pools, a lake, and in the winter, skiing. We, as a family, always enjoy hanging out at the resort with so much to do.

I am forever grateful for my first trip to the Dells and Christmas Mountain; it is here that I fell in love with kayaking. The lake at Christmas Mountain is not large by any means, probably better stated as a pond. But it is in this pond that I rented and paddled my first kayak.

I was hooked! We all were. Paddling all around the pond, through and around the weeping willow tree, with no fear of flipping like a canoe. Peaceful, relaxing, enjoying the sunshine, it made for a perfect new hobby. I bought my own kayak about a week after getting home from that first trip to Wisconsin and have paddled so many places since. So, to the Wisconsin Dells, if nothing else, thank you for introducing me to this wonderful sport.

Food in the Dells isn't a real priority for us. Normally, since there are so many of us when we go, food that we cook ourselves in the cabin is where our priority lies. Your typical "feed an army" foods, chili, spaghetti, burgers and dogs for dinner and Lunchables or "vacation bologna" for lunch. In case your family isn't as "fancy" (aka as weird) as us, vacation bologna is deli sliced bologna and it's only bought on special occasions like vacation, hints the name "vacation bologna". Kind of like going to a fancy steak restaurant because you're out of town but instead it's fancy sliced "meat" for sammiches. You know, the same but more redneck.

On the rare occasions of going out to eat the multiple times we've traveled to Wisconsin, only two places have stood out to me.

One being The Riverside Pub. It's got great American food, and awesome riverside views for dinner. What put it over the top for me and Lisa, the homemade French Onion dip! I don't even remember what I ordered for dinner, but I do remember that it came with homemade potato chips and homemade French Onion dip. So creamy and good, with the perfect amount of onion, it puts all other store bought to shame. If you ever go, get the dip, and bring me some.

The second place may be a bit surprising. I feel ridiculous even saying this. You are going to think this is made up for two reasons. One of the best Mexican restaurants I've ever eaten at was in the Wisconsin Dells. The only other Mexican food that I've had that was better, was in Texas and well of course Mexico.

While looking for somewhere for the seven of us to eat that would please everybody we told my niece, Emily, to see if she could find a Mexican restaurant. Everyone likes Mexican. Born and ready she whips out the Google Maps and starts searching. She says she found one and it's not too far from Walmart, which we needed to go get more vacation bologna anyway so that's convenient. She gives us the directions and we pull in the parking lot.

I said there were two reasons you would think this is made up. Well, we pull in the parking lot and the sign says Kimberly Mexican Restaurant and Store. I kid you not. A Mexican restaurant named Kimberly. Whatever, it's fine, don't judge a book by its cover right. Yeah well, we walk in the front door of this so called "Mexican" restaurant and we are greeted with a grocery store. I know that I was giving Em the "what have you taken us to" look, as were some of the others in the group. We asked for a table and was led between the shelves of packaged corn tortillas and canned tamales. Needless to say, I didn't have a lot of faith in this place. I am woman enough to admit, I was wrong. The food here was amazing. Em, you have my apologies.

Ever since that day, we have trusted Emily to find us a restaurant to eat. Whether in St. Louis or a town we are new to. She has this uncanny ability to find a good and unique place to eat. It may not be the ability to fly or turn invisible, but it's a pretty cool superpower.

Since we are discussing food and Wisconsin, let's talk about the elephant in the room.

Cheese.

I am personally Team Cheese. I know, I know, it's a love it or hate it food group. I love cheese, my mother loves cheese, my sister loves cheese. My niece Issy cannot stand it. Everyone has their quirks; we love her anyway.

There is a small corner on the "strip" of the Wisconsin Dells, where all the souvenir shopping is along with restaurants and booths to buy different tours, it has a Bavarian vibe to it. You know the look, like something you would see in old world Germany or France, think the opening scene of *The Beauty and the Beast* where Belle is singing around town. This is where I was introduced to an insane amount of cheese!

I know there is a lot of cheese in the world and if I was to go to Europe, I'm sure my mind would be even more blown. This place had a lot of cheese, cheeses I've never even heard of. More importantly, though, this is where we learned about the cheese curd. It's small, it's delicious, and it squeaks!

That's right, squeaks.

Apparently, per the lady in the Carr Valley Cheese Co., if a cheese curd squeaks when you eat it, it's the freshest! I figured she was screwing with us, but no, it really does make the tiniest little sound when you chew it, like a Styrofoam cup in the cupholder of a Jeep.

If you are team cheese, I recommend the cheese curds. Go get some squeaky deliciousness.

WISCONSIN DELLS, WI

This is gonna sound surprising.

I've been to the "Waterpark Capital of the World" multiple times.

I've only been to a waterpark there...once.

Wisconsin Dells has so many water parks it's hard to pick which one to visit. Mt. Olympus, Noah's Ark, Kalahari, Chula Vista, Great Wolf Lodge, and that's just off the top of my head. They are everywhere.

We visited Mt. Olympus. We were given discounted tickets by our resort so thankfully we didn't have to choose. We unfortunately chose the wrong day to go, that may be what scarred us from going back. We had a great time, don't get me wrong. The waterslides were abundant and massive, enough to make Six Flags look like the local pool. Plus, Mt. Olympus is also a theme park. So, while the others in the group went off to enjoy the wave pool, excuse me, Poseidon's Rage, and the water slides, one aptly named Tritons Rage, Brenden and I went on to ride the roller coasters.

The problem with the day we went, wasn't the crowds, although not really a fan of crowds, and it wasn't the park itself. It was the weather. While perfect for riding roller coasters, not so perfect for outdoor waterparks. While there is an indoor waterpark which was much warmer and just as fun, all of the said crowds thought so too.

Brenden and I enjoyed the roller coasters way more than the others enjoyed freezing in the waterslides. Zeus, Hades, Cyclopes, (obvious Greek mythology theme in case you missed it) we made trips to each one multiple times, with no plans in stopping. That was until Brenden gets up out of the seat on the Hades 360 and says, "Where's my phone?"

"You are joking right?"

"No! It was in my pocket when we got on the ride." Straight panic creeping onto his face. The last thing his Mom, my sister, said to us before we left them at the lockers that store all of one's valuable things, so they, you know, don't get wet or damaged or thrown off a roller coaster, is "Hey, why don't you put your phone in the locker, so you don't drop it off a roller coaster?"

"No. Mom. It's fine." In typical teenage boy fashion, like that was the most ridiculous idea she's ever had.

You see the need for panic now.

By the grace of God, the kid running the ride said he saw it fall and he would try to go find it on his break. He found it and thankfully, Lisa was only a little mad when we told her the story of the flying phone. It still worked too.

One of the reasons that we don't visit the waterparks when we go to the "waterpark capital" is we enjoy "water parks" of a different kind.

Wisconsin is a favorite of ours for outdoor fun, and we've only been to one city there.

The Dells is a stone's throw from three large lakes and the Wisconsin River, which runs directly through downtown. The greenery, the cliffs, the water, it's all incredibly beautiful!

When visiting we have always made time for three things – Devils Lake State Park, Mirror Lake State Park, and a boat cruise on the Wisconsin River. Honestly, I don't know which one is my favorite.

Mirror Lake, only about a 15-minute drive from downtown, and Devils Lake, about a 25-minute drive, have many of the same great attractions, forrest, hiking trails, camping, and obviously-lakes. Though they seem to offer the same things, they are greatly different.

Mirror Lake was created from the building of a dam on Dells Creek. The lake winds naturally with the surrounding land, creating "fingers" through the sloping terrain, and it makes for beautiful scenery. It is a no-wake lake, meaning that boats cannot travel above idle speed. Don't let that discourage you from getting out on the lake, sometimes slow is best.

One afternoon we got brave and decided to rent a pontoon boat at Mirror Lake.

Do any of us own a boat at home? Nope.

Do any of us know how to drive a boat? Also, nope.

Do any of us have a boating license? I don't really need to answer that do I.

Well, none of that stopped us. It's idle speed, what could go wrong? I was chosen to "man the helm" of this ship, so to say. I, being the only one who had a micron of experience. Once when my stepdad let me drive his speed boat on Kentucky Lake, I was promptly relieved of those duties mere minutes after taking control. But that was still more experienced than any of the others had combined.

If you are wondering how or why the Wisconsin State Park System let us rent a boat with no experience and no license, they didn't know those things. Apparently in the state of Wisconsin, if you are born on or before January 1, 1989, you are grandfathered in and do not require a boating license.

"Oh, that's great, I'm grandfathered into a boating license then." That's what I told the girl handing out the keys to the pontoon. Not exactly true.... Ok not true at all. I was born before February 1, 1989, which seemed close enough to us. And no, I did not lie about my birthday on a legal document, or to the girl working. Technically, I wrote the correct date on the forms and handed her my real driver's license. So, either she was a dunce, or she simply didn't care because she handed me the keys and said to have a great time!

We did have a great time! We cruised throughout the lake just enjoying the sunshine and scenery. We anchored the boat in a spot we hoped was deep enough for a swim without touching the muddy bottom. No matter how brave and "grown-up" you are, I use that term very lightly because I may be at a "grown-up" age, but, I am not a real "grown-up". Jumping into a lake and touching the bottom will always creep me out, and if you say it doesn't bother you, you are either lying or haven't seen enough horror movies. Contrary to many other trips on boats or otherwise, this one went well, no problems, everyone survived, and no damage to the boat. This might inspire me to get a real boating license. Some day.

Devils Lake, both the lake and the state park itself is much larger. Devils Lake, shaped more like a bowl, is not man made, but made by God and glaciers. It's a beautiful lake that offers beaches, swimming, and my new favorite thing-kayaking! This lake sits at the bottom of amazing cliffs which grant you some amazing views if you take the hike to the top.

Devils Lake is an all-day adventure for us. Pack a couple of coolers and a change of clothes and stay to our hearts content. The plan is usually finding a spot to park, not always easy because it is a very popular park, hike a trail, eat lunch and then play in the lake. When we have finally wore ourselves out, we of course check out the gift shop, gotta get that customary t-shirt and/or coffee mug.

We have visited Devil's Lake every year we visited Wisconsin except once. That was because it was December. Too cold for this girl and everyone else to do any hikes or water sports. Every year we choose the same hiking trail to go on because the views are spectacular. Every year we get lost on this same trail.

EVERY. YEAR.

I always think, we won't get lost this time, we are familiar with it now. I'm proven wrong every time. We don't have to call in "Search and Rescue" or anything that dramatic. We eventually find our way out, but you would think with the possibly hundreds of other people taking the same trail, we could just follow them, but, no, we did that once and that's how we got lost the first time. So, our lack of direction isn't always our fault. Maybe one year we will just take a different trail, or I don't know, maybe not get lost on the same freaking trail for the umpteenth time!?! I'll keep you posted.

Another favorite water activity of ours is the Wisconsin River. It is beautiful. You'll notice I say that about most water features, I'm a water person. It really is beautiful, it snakes its way in and around downtown, giving you the opportunity to see its beauty from the Riverside Walk, a drive through town, or a close hiking trail. The best views however, come from either hiking, or one of the Dells Boat Tours. I haven't had the chance to kayak the Wisconsin River yet but it's on my list for next time, right alongside "don't get lost at Devils Lake".

A recommended hiking trail for a view of the Wisconsin River, that isn't too far from town, is the Chapel Gorge Trail. It's only a 5-minute drive from downtown, and it is an easy loop trail that is less than 2 miles long with very pretty scenery. It was summertime when we hiked so everything was in full green contrasting the major rock and sandstone formations, and the small descent down to the beach of the Wisconsin River to the cool waters was welcomed.

If you aren't a hiker, although Chapel Gorge Trail could almost be considered an adventurous walk, consider Dells Boat tours instead, or in addition to the hike.

The first year, we ventured out on the Upper Dells tour, which just means it travels above the Kilbourn Dam. You get fantastic views of the river that was glacier carved, and the many sandstone rock formations. If you have luck like us and a monsoon of a rainstorm will start as soon as you set sail. Don't worry there is an inside cabin to stay dry. Or if you are even more like us, a place to warm up after you've been soaked through, because you thought *it was just a little rain and it's June, it'll be fine*. It wasn't fine and by the end of it we were soaked and cold, I hate being cold.

Our second cruise with the Dells Boat Tours was by far my favorite. A lot of that had to do with the fact that it wasn't raining. Although a little rain and thunder may have made this tour even more fun.

The Ghost Boat. So creepy, so fun!

This tour also takes you around the same areas of the Upper Dells Tour, but it's after dark and the spookiness is on high. Haunted house, haunted hayride vibes, but on water. This tour was my younger niece's idea, she was around 10 at the time. Ten may be a bit young for a haunted boat ride, but it was her idea, and she did nickname herself "Mad Dog", so we didn't figure she'd be scared of anything. Well, that may have been a little misguided.

The tour includes a stop at Witches Gulch, a narrow carving through rock formations with a wooden walkway, because the moss and lichen covered rock walls weren't disturbing enough, we have to walk on a creaky wooden path. You continue your spooky narrated tour on foot, you walk the lantern lit path through the canyon and forest. Water dripping slowly from every rock ledge. They do not cheat you on creepy props and adrenaline inducing scare tactics. The sounds you hear, or think you hear, are magnified from barely being able to see. My niece was not prepared for the "jump factors" about haunted tours. Lurking around every corner is someone or something ready to surprise you with fear. Mad Dog spent the entire tour, almost in tears, but trying to be a mad-dog and not cry. She was attached to mine or Lisa's arm, nails digging in our forearms, wanting, begging it to be over! Unfortunately for her that wasn't an option, she had to "mad-dog-up" and just endure it.

When we got back to the dock and the tour was over, she said "That was really fun! We should do that again next time!" Oh "Mad Dog" you silly thing!

The Dells are full of fun things to do, for everyone. Like I said earlier nothing screams family vacation more than The Dells. You have your typical tourist things, Ripley's Believe It or Not, Wax Museums, Mini-Golf, and Go-Carts, but does have its own set of unique shows and stops too.

The Wisconsin Deer Park is a must. Located in downtown, it is just as the name says, a park full of deer. Not some boring drive through park, but a full-on Snow White experience. This beautiful park allows you and your family to walk around the grounds of the "zoo" with deer just everywhere. Some are in the enclosures, and some just follow you around, like you are Snow-freaking-White. Deer of all kinds, some native to the Americas and some not. They will curiously nosey up to you, eating feed and ice cream cones straight from your hands. Some simply don't care about you and just lounge around, in the grass, in the walking path, in the snack booth, whatever they are feeling. It is so much fun for the whole family and should not be missed.

My first-time zip-lining was in Wisconsin Dells. There are a few different choices of companies to go with. Bigfoot Zip lines was where we went on our first zip line excursion. Easy access, right in town, but with plenty of great nature filled lines to travel on, even one crossing a large water feature. They give you all the ins and outs of ziplining before you start and even give you a tutorial on "tricks" you can do on the photo-op line. I chose the hanging upside down option. Which is way fun and can give you a major head rush and even better adrenaline bump. Best high there is. Brenden chose the "no hands- show off the guns" and Lisa, also chose to go upside-down. Yeah, the one afraid of heights went ziplining, and not just ziplining but upside-down ziplining... anything for her baby-boy!

One of my most memorable parts of the zip line trip had nothing to do with zip-lining, it was when the zip line instructor referred to Lisa as my Mom! Brenden and I got very wide-eyed, looked directly at each other with sheepish grins, lips pinched and did our best not to laugh. With one look at Lisa, her eyes ablaze, we couldn't hold it in. I'm not sure who she wanted to deck more, us for laughing or that poor girl for calling her my mother. No worries though, no one got hit, but we do get a flick in the skull whenever we bring it up. Totally worth it.

A couple years later, on a trip to The Dells, Brenden and I wanted to go zip-lining again and have some fun on our own. The kiddos in the group weren't all that into the idea of flying through the woods strapped to a steel cable with just some canvas straps, carabiners, and a bike helmet. It's a little more in depth than that but to a kid that's all it looks like. So, we went just me and him and tried out Vertical Illusions zip lines.

This tour is a lot more private, and not just the area. The group sizes are smaller, and the zip lines themselves are more secluded. It is the companies private land as well, so you aren't allowed to take your own camera or Gopro, but they will gladly take them for you. You can zip through the dense ecosystem with no sound pollution from the city because the shuttle to the zip lines is 20 minutes. You are out of town and into God's green earth!

We had a great time with both, so either way I don't think you could go wrong. Unless you are someone who referred to my sister as my mother, then you are wrong, very wrong.

The year of 2020 sucked for everyone. People got sick, schools and businesses shut down, and vacations were canceled. That was no different for us. Lisa, Mom, and I work in healthcare. We were given front row seats to the train wreck that was 2020. In my completely bias opinion, no one needed a vacation more than every single healthcare worker in the world that year. Every. Single. One.

That year at Christmas, we had to shift our plans like everyone else. No cruise for us that year, we spend 12 hours a day, or night in my case, wearing a mask. We were not going to spend our vacation doing that too. So, we chose Wisconsin for our Christmas vacation. Just one week, of no worries, no problems, no masks and time together. Even if it was in the cold and snow, and not our usual, we were going to make the best of it.

Make the best of it we did. As for the no worries, no problems, that was a pipe dream.

We had problems before we even left Missouri.

Three days before we left, I threw my back out. I was in so much pain, I couldn't move. I laid on my couch, frozen, begging the pain to be gone in an hour, then in the next hour, then by morning. Finally, I couldn't take it. I called my Mom, aka my doctor, and told her the problem. She told me what to do and I made an appointment with the chiropractor to hopefully fix it. It was better by the time we left but definitely still in a lot of pain.

Two days before we left my grandpa called Mom telling her he couldn't breathe. He was 88 at the time, a heart attack and stroke survivor and a former smoker, so being out of breath wasn't necessarily an unnatural occurrence for him, but calling my Mom about it was. Like most families, we took our precautions with germs and especially with the older folks to avoid getting or giving them COVID. After some convincing and a trip to the ER, come to find out grandpa did have COVID pneumonia, and was going to be admitted to the hospital.

After seeing first-hand what happens to the older community when it came to COVID, we were on edge, and unsure about what to do. Mom told us to go on without her, she needed to be home. Even though no one was allowed to visit COVID patients in those early days, Mom couldn't stand the thought of being in a different state. That's not how we roll though. Lisa and I didn't want to leave Mom or grandpa, and travel hundreds of miles away while he was so sick and she a nervous wreck. So, my bro-in-law called our resort told them we would be late if we came at all, family emergency.

We didn't need to worry so much. That man was tough as nails. Mom talked to him multiple times on the phone, and he was doing just fine.

Terrorizing the nurses and other workers, and showing off how stubborn he could be, his orneriness will always be one of my favorite qualities of him.

Two fairly major problems and vacation hadn't even started.

So, after much debate and conversations with family it was decided we should go ahead with our vacation, just a little later than planned.

This year was definitely different. We were heading to the cold for Christmas vacation instead of the beach. We chose something with less crowds, we were more stressed, and we added a toddler to the group.

That year we had nine people in our team, ranging from 2 to 62. We had people sleeping everywhere. Kids on pullout couches, kids on air mattresses, I was bunking with my Mom, it was a mad house. Issy and Emily were troopers and volunteered to sleep on air mattresses. Unfortunately, the electric pump was back in Bonne Terre, so we all took turns blowing up both twin sizes with a bike pump, and it took over an hour to get them inflated. It was a mess.

The only new adventure we went on that year was snow-tubing at Cascade Mountain. Our resort wasn't quite up and running for the ski season, for various reasons. We took the short drive to Cascade Mountain, for some tubing rides down the snow.

I was still in a bit of back pain, but I was not missing out. I downed four ibuprofen and a steroid and strapped in. What a blast! I am not a fan of cold, but if it is going to be cold, I want some snow. Feast or famine for me when it comes to winter. We went down the side of that mountain more times than I cared to count, in every combination possible. Single, hooked to someone else, racing each other, backwards, forward, whatever. From 2 to 62 we all flew down that mountain. My two-year-old niece loved it. She sat in her tube without a care in the world, enjoying the ride and all the people watching, giant grin poking out from under her binky. My Mom enjoyed it just as much as any of the kids. We were all laughing and enjoying a few hours of not having to worry about anyone.

The brother-in-law made our resort reservations for Sunday to Sunday, to which we had to change to Monday to Sunday. To our surprise, that Saturday afternoon there was a light rap on our cabin door followed with "housekeeping".

That's odd, we thought, we didn't order any extra towels, nor do we need anything cleaned. Doug opens the door and politely tells the girl that we were all set and didn't need anything, she apologizes and says she thought we had checked out earlier. No big deal, we went about our game of Yahtzee. Then a slightly more adamant knock on the door. Doug answers again, this time to a security guy, we are told that we were supposed to have checked out at noon, why are we still here?

After some discussion, and both men thinking they are in the right, as most men do, turns out Doug accidentally booked us for Sunday to Saturday. First, we arrive late and now we are getting kicked out early?!!

We had to vacate, in an hour!

Do you know how much crap nine people pack in for a week vacation!?

We were in a mad scramble. People going everywhere trying to track down all their belongings. Trying to cram everything back into the vehicles with absolutely no organization. If it fits, it sits. We were throwing away all of our leftovers, because lasagna doesn't travel well. The girls had to deflate their beds, which took a fraction of the time it took to get them set up. We are doing all of this while also trying to wrangle a two-year old and not let her escape.

Absolute chaos.

Doug was finally able to get a hold of someone that dealt with reservations and he explained our situation. They were very accommodating and thankfully allowed us to stay.

So, we more calmly went back to the cars and took out all of our stuff, thinking how well we handled that mass exodus situation. Should the need for an quick evacuation ever arise again, we are all well rehearsed. The poor girls though decided that sleeping on the floor would be less annoying than trying to blow the air mattresses back up.

We still had a great time. Spending time with each other, playing cards, cooking dinner, playing trivia, walking around the resort in the snow, and of course evacuation drills. Just out here making lemonade.

Were we worried about grandpa? Yes.

Did I want to crawl into the fetal position and not move because my back hurt so bad?

Yes.

Were we evicted from our home away from home, in a mass exodus?

Yes.

Were we and the entire world inconvenienced (to say the least) with the spread of this disease?

More than yes.

Did we still have a great time together?

You better believe it. I will say this till I'm blue in the face- fun does not mean perfect! Perfection is way overrated. We have laughed at the story of our frantic eviction from that vacation more times than I can count. It was the core memory from that trip, and it was also one of the biggest mishaps from that trip.

So never, under any circumstances, think that just because things don't go as planned, it won't be exciting or a cherished memory.

Chapter 11
Close to Home

Sometimes even the smallest of trips can have the biggest impact. Welcome to The Saint Francois River.

We are a water loving family. Swimming in the lake or at the pool, lounging by the ocean, going on a cruise, fishing, catchin' crawdads in the creek, canoeing, kayaking, or paddleboarding down the river, you name it and each one of us have done all those things and more.

Since we all love the water and outdoors so much, my sister and her husband decided to invest in some river property. They ended up purchasing property right on the banks of the St. Francois River. This river runs through southeast Missouri, eventually dumping into the Mississippi River, making its way in and around the granite and rhyolite rocks that blanket the area.

It's only around 30 minutes from home, but it is a nice, secluded spot to relax and enjoy nature that doesn't take all day to get to. Sometimes we'd camp there for the weekend, sometimes just go for the day. Our spot sits down a steep gravel road, in a holler right on the river just north of the highway 72 bridge. It has a good stretch of flat land right by the river for a perfect hangout and camping spot. This section in the river also has some deeper spots in it great for catching some fish, either by boat or from the bank.

In 2016, the family and I decided we would take a big float trip down the St. Francois with our kayaks. We planned it all out so that anyone who wanted to go could. Everyone was in. Lisa, The Doug, B, Em, Issy, and I, and even Brenden's then girlfriend joined in on the adventure. We packed lunches, snacks, Gatorade, and waters, borrowed extra kayaks, paddles and life jackets, loaded up the cars and headed to the drop point.

We picked Syenite Access as our drop-in point and the float would end at the family's riverside property. We were in no rush; this wasn't going to be a race of any kind just a nice family kayaking trip before the summer was over and the kids went back to school. The float was going to be just shy of 10 miles, and by our calculations... okay so I'll take the hit for this one... by *MY* calculations, this trip would take us about 8 hours. That gave us a paddling rate of a little over a mile an hour which I thought was slow for us. We had been floating a lot in our kayaks, so I was guesstimating off those trips. I had it figured we would be at the property no later than 8 o'clock pm. That gave us ten whole hours of fun...

Boy was I way off.

The day we picked turned out to be perfect. As usual, in a Missouri August, it was going to be hot and humid all day. Overcast skies eventually clearing off in the evening, but there was no chance of rain, so no sun beating down on us all day. Couldn't have asked for better weather.

We get to the drop off point first. This part is a bit of a hassle, between seven people and seven kayaks plus all the stuff that goes with it, we took two trucks. We drop off the kayaks at Syenite and then Brenden and The Doug go drop off one vehicle at the end point, our river property.

Finally, after all the carpooling, we are ready to shove off!

It was picture-perfect. Beautiful skies, beautiful river, my team is with me, and we are doing what we love.

That is until, we hit our first set of rapids. We aren't even a mile down river, and we already have hit a problem. A problem that would really throw this trip into "thrilling".

Did I mention that the St. Francois River is known for Whitewater Kayak competitions? The geology of this river makes it perfect for Whitewater Kayakers to test their skills and speed, while trying to be the fastest and, of course, to not flip. Dotted with rock boulders of all sizes, and shut-ins causing rapids and rivulets up and down the course of this winding river. It makes for a great route for these professionals to show off.

Now the section we choose for our family float is not part of the competition area. We are not that stupid or that experienced. That does not mean the section of river we are on is all sunshine and rainbows. The Saint is littered with rapids ranging anywhere from class I to class III.

We hit our first set of small rapids, and we all start weaving our way down the drops through various pathways the rocks had created. I had paddled The Saint before, so had Brenden and Lisa, none of this landscape was new to us. We were having a great time, splashing, twisting, and turning through the water, making sure we didn't lean into it enough to tip, then turning our boats around to watch the rest of the crew do the same.

That wasn't the case for Em. Her boat flipped on the very first attempt. She was 12 years old, and this was her first big float trip on a kayak. When her boat flipped, she started to panic, thinking that she would be stuck in it and dragged under the water. Even though she had a life jacket on, the sudden rush of water into her kayak caused a slight freak out. Upon seeing Em's situation, Issy also turned over her kayak, she was 11 and very petite, she ended up sliding right out of the boat as soon as it turned over. We immediately paddle back upriver to check on them, The Doug paddling downriver to them. They are soaking wet, a little anxious but no injuries, other than maybe their pride.

This caused a couple of hang ups. One, we had to get the girls calmed down and help them realize that nothing bad had happened. They were not in danger; we were all here and knew what to do. The water we were in was only a few feet deep, and they had life jackets on. Secondly, we now had two kayaks full of water, and no gravel bars in site. With two boats that are now mostly sunk and nowhere to pull over to empty them, we had to make the girls walk/swim down the river for a bit. Still no gravel bars, or a place in the banks where we could easily stand a couple kayaks up to empty the water, we had to improvise. Brenden finds the biggest flat rock in the river, only about the size of a couch cushion. He drags one of the kayaks to it and with every bit of strength we had started emptying it. It took me, The Doug, and Brenden to empty just one boat. The whole ordeal took us at least 30 minutes to remedy.

Thus, you see where I messed up. When factoring how long this trip would take us, I did not plan on having multiple 30-minute bailing sessions.

After that initial *Titanic* moment, we had many other flips and turnovers causing massive amounts of water to flood our boats. I even flipped my own kayak once. I was so irritated with myself after I did it too, I immediately dragged my kayak back upriver above the drop (when I say drop, I'm only talking like 1-2 feet max, let's not get crazy) that I flipped on and went down it again. This time with much better results.

Even with all the stops along the float we were having a great time. Enjoying ribbing each other every time we crashed, cheering the younger girls on when they went down a rapid with no problems. They were catching on quick. Learning how to turn the boat through faster running water and how to right themselves when hitting a hidden rock under the water. The capsizing was happening less, but we still had problems randomly.

We had a good time teasing The Doug about his "low rider" kayak. His boat took on water easily and ended up sitting very low in the river, caused by a missing drain plug in the back. He had to use a water gun as a makeshift bilge pump for most of the trip. I got a great video of Lisa coming down some rapids and somehow running her kayak right up onto a rock, like she was landing the *Mayflower*. She even gave us the Forest Gump wave after she did like she meant to do that all along. We were having a blast!

We had stopped for a break after we had been on the water for about five or six hours already. Mostly to rest our arms, grab a snack and recoup from draining gallons of water out of our kayaks. That in of itself is exhausting. I decided to check the map on my phone to see how close we were to our end point.

Yes, I take my phone on float trips, I always take my phone, and after this I always will, for a couple of reasons. One to take pictures with, secondly for the map, and third for emergencies. I also had a couple of waterproof walkie-talkies just for the heck of it. I'm not sure even why I threw those in the dry bag. Just on a whim I thought they would be fun. We had no reason to bring them, we were going to all stay together. Thank God I did.

After studying where we were in relation to the endpoint, I was getting concerned but not particularly worried. We still had quite a ways to go and only a few hours left of daylight. I mentioned, nonchalant, to Lisa that we still had a lot further to go, more than I thought we should for how long we had been on the water. We both thought about it, but shrugged it off, we still had a couple hours of daylight left, and there wasn't much we could do but keep trucking along.

We should've been more concerned.

Dark starts approaching. We still have miles to go. We are in the middle of nowhere.

The trip started to get real uncomfortable, real fast. When dusk hits us, we are in a section of river where we had to drag our boats due to the shallow water and the number of rocks. It's here that my sister's kayak somehow gets caught in just enough current to get pulled away from her, turning over, losing a cooler and her paddle in the process. We can barely see with the now near absent sunlight. We only found her kayak because it was bright orange, and it was stopped by a downed tree across the river. We never did recover the cooler or her paddle.

We then get to a portion of river deep enough to sit in our kayaks. We hop in hoping to get down the river at a faster pace than walking. That was taking twice as long. The girls were losing their sandals, the kayaks kept getting hung on rocks or branches that we couldn't see. So, we decided to paddle again. Problem was we were one paddle short, and the sun had completely disappeared. To make matters worse the moon was just a sliver in the sky giving us no illumination.

I make sure to pack exactly four things in my dry box when going kayaking. My phone, a knife, Band-Aids, and Benadryl. I have never thought to pack a flashlight, because I have never planned on being in my kayak after dark. A mistake I will never make again.

Deciding to get back in the kayaks turned out to be a mistake. Bumping into everything and once again flipping, once again having to dump water from our boats. So, we try walking them down river again. All seven of us walking our kayaks, with just the faintest bit of moonlight, was difficult and scary. We couldn't see when the river current was about to pick up speed, nor when a set of rocks and boulders were coming up on us. Unfortunately, both of those happened at the same time.

Doug was in the lead, slightly hunched over dragging his kayak behind him, when the back end of the kayak catches the river current, spins, and knocks him directly into a row of large rocks that came up shin high on him. It was like a derailing train.

One after the other, our kayaks caught that same bit of current. After realizing what happened to Doug we let go of our boats. The problem was he was still up against those rocks, when they all come crashing into the backs of his legs knocking him off balance and causing one foot to get caught between two rocks. This turned his leg in a wrong angle. How his leg didn't break is beyond me. That was truly God looking out for us.

We decided at this point we were going to have to make some changes on how to get down the river. We needed to get serious. We couldn't risk anyone getting hurt to the point of not being able to continue. We had no service and weren't near any accessible roads that we knew of. We were going to have to work our way down the river the best we could until we either got to the property or we simply could not go on. If we got to that point, we would sleep in our kayaks on the riverbank until daylight. Something none of us wanted but...

We decided to make the younger girls and Brenden's girlfriend stay in their kayaks. The four of us then strapped our boats to theirs with the carabiners we had and walked them down the river. Bless them, they sat in the kayaks not making a sound unless asked. They were so helpful in that simple way. The four of us were very stressed out, wore out, and worried. Them not complaining or voicing how scared they were is what kept us from losing our minds completely.

My phone thankfully still had a bit of battery, so I entrusted Em with the navigation.

Side note: If you ever find yourself going on a trip, whether it be a camping trip or a vacation or whatever, download an "offline map" of the area you are going to with google maps or any GPS map that is capable. Even if you are going to the city, trust me it could save you.

Since cell service was shoddy in that area, I had downloaded one of the area the first time I had made the drive to the property, and it had been stored on my phone ever since. So, I instructed Em to watch the blue dot on the map, that was us, and to watch the blue line of the river. She had to tell us when we were coming up on a turn and which direction the river was heading. She navigated like a champ. She knew when to keep the phone on to watch the river and when to conserve battery. Super proud of the maturity she showed then.

Remember when I said, "thank God I brought those walkie talkies". Well, here is why. I'm not sure how we figured this out, but these little life savers had built in flashlights!! We all took turns with one, whoever was in front usually had the light on them. We decided to only use one at a time to save battery in case we had to spend all night out on the river. They weren't a huge amount of light, they only had one tiny LED bulb each, but that was enough to lift our spirits some.

That was until we realized what all we could see, now that we had light.

Glowing eyes on the riverbanks of creatures we couldn't name, ripple trails in the water of seemingly still portions of river caused by animals I didn't want to think about, innumerable bugs attracted to the light attacking whoever was lighthouse at that moment. Fish attacking us every chance they had, thank God piranhas aren't native to Southeast Missouri. The uplift we got from having some illumination was dwindling with every creepy shadow exposed in this river.

It was nearing midnight. We were all mentally drained, thinking this couldn't get any worse. We are all mostly quiet aside from the occasional exasperated sigh and our "check-ins" we would make randomly.

"Everyone here?"

"Yup."

"Yeah."

"Still here."

"Girls?"

"Yup, we're good."

We had to call out to each other to make sure we hadn't lost anyone. Even though we could hear each other in the water and faintly see with the little bit of light we had, we didn't want to take any chances of someone getting lost. We had enough problems.

It's at this point I'm starting to realize I am more or less swimming the boats down the river. I can no longer touch, except for the occasional rock underwater that I can get a foot on, I am no longer any help in getting the boats down river. Not good. Being the shortest of the family, no one was surprised or upset with my now lack of help. However, soon Lisa was also not able to touch the riverbed, now swimming, and then Doug was swimming with us. Brenden was now the only one able to touch the bottom of the river, with only his head and neck out of water, he is now solely dragging seven kayaks and six people down river. The three of us kicking our legs trying to help as much as possible but with so much exhaustion I'm not sure how much I helped. This is why he refers to this trip as our "Seal Team 6" kayak trip. It was at this moment we seriously contemplated an overnight camp on the banks.

We are finally in a water level that we can now all walk and pull kayaks with more ease. We discussed if we should continue, when Em exclaims "I think the property is right around this corner!!"

She hands me the phone, and by golly we are!! We have one more bend in the river before we are on the straight stretch in front of our property. That good news gives us a little kick and we push to the end with a little more energy than we had the last few hours.

It took everything I had not to kiss the ground when we finally pulled the last kayak up on the bank. I had never been so happy to be out of the river. We made it. Bruised, battered, exhausted and very hangry but we made it. It was now 1 a.m. and we were heading home to a hot shower and a warm bed.

The Doug said screw the kayaks we can come back and get them another day. Well, actually what he said was a lot more colorful and something about he didn't care if he ever saw those kayaks again.

When we got back to Syenite access and to Brenden's truck, I got out to ride with him and his girlfriend.

"Brenden, you take her home and Amber home, then we'll see you back at the house. Okay?" Lisa tells him.

"ABSOLUTLEY NOT!" he said with a sternness in his voice I had never heard before. "I am not taking my girlfriend back to her dad's house at 1 a.m. when I told him we would be back by 10 without one of you there with me!" on the verge of panic, thinking about having to face her ex-military dad and explain coming home at one in the morning.

"Hmm... yeah, I guess you are right, probably should come with you."

Mistakes were made on this trip. We learned a few things the hard way. And there were times I wasn't sure we would make it home unharmed. It was quite the adventure though. One of the exciting ones you get to tell your uncles and cousins all about at Thanksgiving dinner.

How we made it out of that river with only a few cuts and bruises is only by the grace of God. We could have been seriously hurt multiple times. We could have been attacked by an animal of some kind, whether it be a coyote, mountain lion, or a snake, with only our hands and a couple of pocketknives to defend ourselves. Had the temperature of the water or air been slightly lower we would have risked hypothermia. I'm pretty sure we were close to being reported as missing to the authorities. Boy, wouldn't that have been embarrassing to see on the news the next day.

As crazy as this trip was, I don't hate it. We learned a lot that trip, and up until the sun setting, we were having a pretty great time. Enough time has passed that I can say I don't regret it. I think it's still too soon for some of the others though.

Chapter 12
Southern Caribbean Cruise

Christmas of 2016, we decided to give a cruise another try. Even after "vomit in the Bahamas" of January 2016, somehow the family was willing to go another round with the deep sea. Everyone except Mom that is. Upchucking all over the breakfast table on the lido deck was something she wasn't quite ready to forget about. So, this year our Christmas cruise was just us siblings and the kiddos.

We chose to leave out of New Orleans this time. Remembering when I went on my first cruise, I didn't notice many people getting sick, so I told Lisa maybe we should give that a try instead of cruising the Atlantic Ocean. We hoped, with the change in sea-nery (see what I did there) and the premedicating with anti-nausea drugs, we would have a little more fun and a little less barf this time.

We chose big this year. Our trip was a 7-night cruise, stopping in Jamaica, Grand Cayman, and Mexico. It was probably one of the smoothest vacations we have been on. We finally got one! The ports were beautiful, the seas were smooth, and the excursions were adventurous.

New Orleans was a take two for me. For everyone else it was new sights and sounds. The French Quarter still had the same smells, the same crowds, and the same drunks frolicking through the streets, but it is an experience, so we went.

We didn't spend too much time there at night, with four kids under the age of 16, we didn't want them to witness too much of the experience. We did give them a little sip of Bourbon Street night life and went for some burgers. That's right we went back to the alligator burger, I had to get another one, and I knew my buddy would want to try it. A 16-year-old football player is basically a human garbage disposal, and he was all for it, he and I do a lot of food adventures in our travels together.

We set sail for Jamaica, which took two sea days, on the *Carnival Dream*. It was already going much better than our first Christmas cruise. The sun was shining and there were no waves at all! Two days at sea can get pretty monotonous, but they schedule lots of activities for the whole family and hey, anything is better than being at work. There's food to eat, games to play, sunburns to get, and trivia to win.

Carnival cruise trivia. Our family, who is not competitive at... ok extremely competitive, will be at every single trivia game hosted. We don't care if we know a thing about the theme of the trivia, we are going.

One particular trivia game was a subject we know very well, 90s music. Let me just start this by saying, we are white, like white white, as Caucasian as they come from the middle of nowhere in the middle of this country. Farmers tans, jeans to church, George Straight and Hank Williams may have been on every local station, but my big sister grew up in the 90s, and who was in charge of me while my Mom worked 12 hours in the ICU? She was! So, do we know all the lyrics to *All My Exes Live in Texas*? Yes, we do. Can we also rap every lyric to *Gangsta's Paradise*? You better freaking believe it. And we made sure all the kids could too. Knowledge that came in very handy during this trivia game and got us one of the best compliments.

We were belting it! Throwing up peace signs as we were "rapping", like we had any idea what a real gangsta did. None the less, when a group of African American women walked by, with some incredible braids I might add, gave a little lean like Chris Tucker on *Friday* and shouted "Daaammmnnnn, them white folks can rap!?!". I felt pretty good about myself for the rest of the day, and every time that song comes on, I remember that day at trivia. The smallest compliment can follow someone the rest of their lives, even if it is more a statement of shock, than an actual compliment.

Our ability to "rap" however, did not secure the win for us.

Ocho Rios, Jamaica was our first port of call. The beautiful people of Jamaica with their beautiful accents welcomed us with open arms and lots of fun.

I don't remember which kid but one of them picked our adventure for the day. Like on all of our other trips we chose to book not with Carnival but with the locals. We were going whitewater rafting! Okay, so it's not quite that extreme. We chose to go on a river tubing excursion.

We went with White River Calypso Rafting. They took us on the, you guessed it, White River. It was stunning. If you are from where I am, you are well versed in the art of a river float. This was not your ordinary float down the river. The river changed every turn with calm flowing greenish blue waters, then quick drops creating the best little rapids for you to slide down. The vibrant green forest surrounded us on both sides of the river, transporting us into a real-life *Jungle Book*. I expected Baloo to come floating down on his back at any moment. It was a perfect adventure and we would do it over again and again.

The river trip took the perfect amount of time to have fun and enjoy, but still left enough time to do some shopping and eating in Ocho Rios. As always, gotta stop for the t-shirt and/or coffee mug. Here we also went for the coffee and rum cake, a staple in any Jamaican souvenir shop.

We walked around looking at the trinkets you can get to remember your vacation with. Jamaicans are a friendly bunch. Offering coffee to sample, which we did. Offering rum cake to try, which we did. One fella even offered to let us sample some rum, so while we were waiting for Doug to find the one and only thing he wanted on this trip, a Bob Marley shirt, we stayed and talked to the rum guy. He hands me a sample, then Lisa a sample, then Brenden a sample, who at 16 years-old, gingerly lifted his hand to take it, trying not to let anyone see.

"Whoa, whoa, whoa!!" Lisa blocks the exchange with the Mom arm motion, "what are you doing?" she asked the rum guy with a laugh, out of surprise not anger. "He's 16!!"

I am certainly enjoying this show, will she let him drink it? Is she going to be mad? My eyes darting from my sister to rum guy to Brenden.

Rum guy looks at us, raises one eyebrow, shrugs the shoulders, and in that beautiful Caribbean drawl says, "You in Jamaica mon!"

"What does that mean? There aren't any age limits to alcohol here?"

"Well, technically...but you in Jamaica mon, you see over da bar, you can 'ave a drink."

Simultaneously, every one of my family members turns to look at me, all 5'2" of me (5'3" with shoes on) and almost like it was rehearsed I hear "Hmm, you just barely make that cut!"

Y'all are flipping hilarious.

After our successful outing of short jokes and underage drinking we move on to our next port. The Grand Cayman Island. I know I say this a lot, but it was beautiful here. Breathtaking. The blue of the water, the white sand, everything seemed so bright and shiny. This beautiful island protects its waters and coral reefs so well. So, to keep everything so bright and shiny and beautiful, the cruise ships don't actually dock. They throw anchor and you use a tender boat, which is just a water taxi, if you will, for large groups of people to get to the island docks.

This was the port I was most looking forward too. We had decided days ago when looking up things to do, what our adventure would be. We were going swimming with stingrays. I couldn't wait. Yes, Steve Irwin was in the back of my mind, but that was a terrible freak accident, one that I hoped wouldn't be repeated. This was definitely one of the coolest excursions I've ever taken.

We had booked this tour online, not with the cruise but with a local. We get to the island and find our tour company. Don't worry, there may be a literal boat load of people all trying to do the same, but the tour companies make it pretty idiot proof to find where you supposed to go. With signs and plenty of instructions we find our group and head out, sun beating down on us, we were ready to see the beautiful waters and wildlife the Cayman's had to offer.

It was a short bus ride to the dock. Loaded up with all the other families out for the same adventure, we boarded the small vessel, bigger than a john boat but smaller than our tender boat. Open sides and benches lining the rails, you could just relax and enjoy the ride, going no faster than an idle it seemed, the ocean gave enough breeze to almost lull you to sleep if you wanted.

The boat ride takes a while to get to where the stingrays hang out. Which may seem like you would be in some pretty deep water going out that far. By the time we got to our destination you could barely see the island. However, in deep water we were not. I could stand up! All 5'2" of me (5'3" with shoes on) could stand up way out here in the ocean! It was incredible. The water still that perfect shade of turquoise blue, yet so clear you could see the bottom sand you were standing in.

When you get to the spot of the stingrays, you are given a few instructions. Mostly so there are no Steve Irwin type scenarios, but also, to keep others and the stingrays themselves safe around you. Don't make a lot of ruckuses, don't chase them, and don't try to grab their stingers, to name a few.

Man's ability to not follow the simplest of directions is uncanny. Almost immediately after we got our "don't do's", we hear behind us a girly screeching scream, followed by a lot of splashing and commotion. As if giving a demonstration on what not to do, a group of morons from another tour boat, decided to chase the stingrays around, provoking them causing them to get fired up and annoyed. The stingrays decided to chase back. We almost got our Steve Irwin moment folks. After some yelling from the Caribbean locals running the show, everything calmed down and no one was hurt.

We got our instructions and demonstration on what not to do, it was now time to know what we could do. We could feed them, let them touch us and even touch them. The guides gave us a small piece of fish and said to hold it in our hands like you would an ice cream cone, with the thumb tucked in so the rays could take the fish and not one of your fingers. Yikes.

I don't know what I expected when feeding these massive fish, I've fed plenty of animals by hand and I've fed fish, but I've never fed a giant fish by hand. It wasn't what I had been expecting. Those guys turn into vacuum cleaners when there is bait in the water! You hold out your pretend ice cream cone filled with fish bait, and then the stingray, its mouth being on the underside, will swim over your hand and just hoover it right out.

It was an incredible feeling having the giant rays come brush against you as they swam by. They were so fluid in their motions, no dramatic splashing and thrashing in the cool blue waters. Never once did we feel in danger.

The beautiful fish weaved in and around our group much like a cat that laces its way gently around its owners legs looking for affection. These giant fish knew what to expect when new boats arrived, snacks and friends. The best way I can explain how a stingray feels is, take your tongue and run it across the inside of your cheek. They are super soft and squishy; they have a slickness to them but not slimy. Definitely not like any fish I've taken off the line before.

We got our customary photos offered by the tour guide. They gave us opportunities to pose with the rays, individually and as a family. The stingray in our group photo, looks like a cartoon character, not sure how he got in this predicament, but it made for a great family photo. The guides even dared a couple of us to give the rays a big ol' fat smooch, so we did!

This was undeniably a vacation for the books. We didn't have any mishaps guys! Well, other than the rum guy trying to get Brenden in trouble for underage drinking.

The Cayman Islands were so stunning, I know I can't wait to get back.

Chapter 13
Caribbean Cruise: Girls Only

The summer of 2017, Lisa and I decided it was time to up the vacation game and go on a cruise during the summer. Not only were we going during a different time of year, we also were going without any parents or kids to supervise us.

My sister and I both have Radiology Degrees. She took hers down an ultrasound path, I took mine down the cat-scan path. Same toolbox, different tools. We both ended up working at the same hospitals, yes plural, we like money, we like vacations, so we have multiple jobs. At my full-time job, she is PRN or "as needed" and at her full-time job, I am PRN or "as needed". Working alongside your sister and best friend is one of life's joys, although it doesn't happen very often, it is so fun when it does.

One day while at work we decided that we needed a girl's trip with our WASHCO work crew. (Her full-time location, my PRN) We got the girls in the department in on our plans and they, of course, were all for it. Who was going to run the radiology department while we were gone, who knows? We'll let the three boys that are left work that out. It's a small hospital and small department, so we all felt like family, spending a week together in close quarters was no big deal to us. We've already been through some traumatic situations together, certainly we could survive some fun in the Caribbean together.

We chose the 5-day Western Caribbean cruise out of New Orleans. A repeat sail for me, but I didn't care. I was just happy to be back in the ocean. Just like my cruise with Katie and Dan, there would be planned stops in Cozumel and Progreso, Mexico.

As expected, even with a different travel crew, the trip couldn't go smoothly. It couldn't even start smoothly. We didn't even leave before we had a hitch. A member of our travel crew had to cancel because of a family emergency, unfortunate but family is and always will be the first priority, something we could all understand. So, we were down to five of us; me, Lisa, Michelle, Kris, and Megan.

We start our trip the same as the others, making the long, painstakingly boring drive down to Louisiana. Miles and miles of Highway 55, through Arkansas, Tennessee, all of Mississippi, and finally into the Bayou.

Kris, Lisa, and I were in one car, Michelle and Megan in another. With all of us able to drive we could switch on and off multiple times just to keep it interesting enough for the driver, and the back seat princess could get a good nap in.

We stopped at a gas station in Mississippi, a grungy little Mom and Pop stop for fuel, a pee break, and snacks. Michelle found some "burnt ends" on the hot plate section and decided they would make a good road trip snack. Well, they must have been God's gift to gas station food because we heard about it for the next four and a half hours.

"Y'all should've got some of them, you don't know what you were missing."

"We are going to stop back at that place on the way home. Those we're so good."

"I bet this gas station doesn't have burnt ends that are as good as that last place!"

Unfortunately, she did go back on the way home, and they were not as good.

We got to NOLA late that night, some of us still dreaming of burnt ends. We had dinner, and went to bed. We aren't big partiers, so we decided to explore the city the next day.

The morning before our ship set off, we did something I had yet to experience. See the French Quarter in the daylight!

NOLA is just as alive during the day. Crowds of people, some more sober, and some more hungover, walk the streets of The French Quarter in much of the same way as they do at night. Taking in the overwhelming sights, sounds, and smells. Senses being attacked in the same way just on the opposite side of the clock-face.

Instead of bar music that's too loud and the bar crowds, it's live jazz in the streets played by the locals, and families laughing and enjoying music and dancing along with everyone. Instead of bright neon lights, it's bright sunshine glinting off the Creole style buildings and of course the yellow, purple, and green beads that are left forgotten or hung from the many iron railings and landscapes around the city. The urine smell, however, never goes away, if anything it gets worse. The humid coastal air drawing it out of the sidewalk crevices, cooking it in the concrete to spread the mighty odor across the neighborhood. If you're lucky enough though you might be able to forget about the urine smell because your nose is being drawn to the fresh coffee and fresh baked Beignets.

One of the most beautiful sights to see in the French Quarter though, that cannot be ignored, is the beautiful Saint Louis Cathedral Church. In the middle of Jackson Square it towers over every building around it, with its massive gray spires piercing the city sky. The two-toned gray exterior looks like it should have gargoyles guarding its high ledges, but instead it is intricately designed iron crosses that keep watch.

The colorful interior of the church is quite the contrast to the exterior. The towering ceiling is decorated with beautiful murals depicting stories of the Bible. From the rafters hang various flags. The stained-glass windows are an unbelievable, mesmerizing beauty all on their own.

Michelle, being one of the few in our group of Catholic faith, lit a prayer candle while we visited. We stood and watched patiently. Gently and quietly she lowered the lighting stick to the candle. A candle lit, whether in memory or in prayer, such a simple gesture, yet there is so much beauty and meaning in it. She is the one in the group that is without a doubt the loudest, most full of life, always ready for a laugh. Yet, I had never seen her so tranquil and quiet, treasuring this peaceful moment. This may seem strange, but I was glad I got to witness this.

Our time on board had its ups and downs. We all got to the port, circling the top deck of the parking garage multiple times trying to find somewhere to squeeze into. They may guarantee a safe and secure parking area, but it does come with a catch, fitting your six-foot-wide car into a six-foot three-inch parking space. We witnessed multiple cars ditching their passengers and luggage in the isle, then park.

In hindsight, we should have unloaded Kris at the door. While walking across the crosswalk into the building, a cabbie thought she was walking too slow and took off before she had made it completely onto the sidewalk. She wasn't hurt physically, by any means; her luggage however, was a different story. Her poor black and white zebra striped roller luggage did not look brand new anymore. It had one bottom corner caved in, the hard plastic and metal frame molding to the weight of the cab. One wheel was sticking out at a wrong angle, and the previously black and white strips now supported a lovely shade of tire tread across the bottom edge. Kris, being Kris, yelled every obscenity she could think of at the cabbie as he drove away, and then a few more under her breath as she limped her bag down the sidewalk.

You tell him Kris!

We got to our staterooms, clunker bag in tow. I mentioned there were originally supposed to be six of us on this trip. Three in one room; three in another. Michelle and Megan, mother and daughter I might add, now had a room to themselves. Not a big deal, they would just have an extra bed in their room, and they were free to be just like they were at home. The three of us remaining still shared a room like we had originally booked from the start.

The problem with that though, we get to the room and there are only two beds. Now most of the time in an interior stateroom, there are places in the ceiling or the upper part of the walls where you can tell that a bunk folds out of. No such places in our room. *Hmm, well they must have given us the wrong room we thought.* We find the nearest worker and ask about the room; she assures us we are in the correct room. *Well, what about the fact that there are 3 grown women staying in here and only 2 twin size beds?* She nonchalantly walks into our room, reaches under one of the twin beds, and pulls out a "cot", to put it generously. She says here is your third bed, thanks us, and leaves us standing there stunned.

We all three were silently glancing back and forth at each other, not saying anything. Being the shortest and the youngest, BY LIKE A LOT, ok so maybe not a lot but more than a couple of years, I already knew how this was going to go. So, I spent the next five nights… on a luxury cruise ship… sleeping on the floor.

Cruise ships, if you've never been on one, are like a floating party all the time. There is always something going on. Deck party dance offs, mixology competitions, trivia, hairy chest contest, ice sculpting, bingo, or simply laying by the pool in a lounge chair being asked "can I bring you anything from the bar?" eleventeen times an hour by the helpful staff. If you get bored on a cruise, that's on you.

I do get that not everyone loves these types of things, like crowds and loud music. Even our own Kris hollered every time we walked out by the pool deck, shaking her head "all this damn loud music!!", making her sound about 80, even had the scrunched eyebrows and whiney rasp that geriatrics tend to use when they don't like something. Something Megan and I noticed immediately and to this day when we see her, we like to just scrunch our faces and imitate her "damn loud music!" back at her.

Our first stop was in Progreso, which sits on the north side of the Yucatán Peninsula. It has next to nothing to do there. Aside from a few souvenir shops, tour booking booths, and transportation to take you out of the port, it doesn't offer much else. That doesn't make it a stop to skip though, fun can be had from this port, just not in the immediate area.

We didn't book anything beforehand for this trip. We knew there wasn't a lot offered here and between the five of us we needed to discuss our options together first. I had already done the Mayan Ruins tour, and I was all for it again, but that's not everyone's cup of tea. We decided on something relaxed and laid back.

So, we landed on a tour of Merida, which is actually the capital of the state of Yucatán. Considered a historical tour, our main attraction was the *Casa Del Montejo*. A 1500s Spanish mansion turned museum. You are met with a beautiful aging stone entryway, that immediately makes it feel as if you are stepping through a time portal into the 16th century.

After a tour of the mansion, we spent a while walking the square, or *Plaza Grande*. Taking in the other equally beautiful buildings, painted in vibrant powder blues, canary yellows, and rusted reds. A massive cathedral church that will amaze you sits on the corner, as well.

We even stopped at a 7-11, although we did not get a Mexican Big Gulp, we did hit the sorbet shop next door. A few of us were slightly concerned with the name, *Dulcería and Sorbetería Colón*. I was assured *Colón* translates to "Columbus" in Spanish, and not "you're about to regret this". Some of the best sorbet I've ever had too, after one bite I didn't care what "*Colón*" meant.

Our tour guide took us to a local restaurant nearby. First, he asked if we wanted to try one of his favorites or go to more of a larger chain restaurant away from the historic area we were in. Thankfully, the others in the group wanted to go to his local favorite because that would have been very disappointing to go to a chain restaurant while in another country. If given the choice **always** go local!

This I knew was going to be some great authentic food because the menu had zero English words on it. I had no idea what I was doing and neither did the other four. With the advice of our guide, I was able to pick out some of the best tacos I have ever had! Fresh homemade corn tortillas, shredded chicken, pickled onions, they were incredible. You may be wondering how I can remember that, being that it was a few years ago, well they were that good!

Our next port was Cozumel. Not mine and Lisa's first visit, or even second. The number of visits doesn't make it any less attractive though. Anytime I can lay on a beach with a bracelet that can get me any drink I want and any food on the menu brought to me, is a good time. No matter how many visits I've made there before.

This was our beach day of the trip. Our plan was to get day passes to a beach club resort, lay in the sand, swim in the beautiful Gulf waters, and enjoy the sunshine.

Let me introduce you to Mr. Sancho's.

This is a small beach club resort about 20 minutes from the cruise terminal, 10 if you get the right taxi driver. (Mom would make a great Mexican taxi driver) For, what I think is a reasonable fee, they will give you a bracelet that gives you full access to their beach chairs, pools, hammock swings, full menu, buffet, and bar! The staff has always been so friendly and accommodating each time I've been. Every time we have a stop in Cozumel, this is where we spend the day.

Like with any beach resort, there are always options for more adventure once you get settled. Parasailing, banana boat tours, snorkeling, and more. Meg and I decided to give parasailing a try while here. The trip was beautiful! Flying high we got great views of the island, the beach, and the deep blue waters of the Caribbean. If you haven't parasailed before I highly recommend. From the ground it might would seem violent, loud, and high on the adrenaline scale. It isn't. It's quiet, serene, and a lot calmer than it would seem. There is a unexpected peaceful silence hundreds of feet in the air. If relaxed adventure is more your style, try parasailing.

Michelle being the people person she is, made friends with some folks by the pool. After chatting with her new friends, Michelle notices their drinks are purple, not something you see very often (not that I have anyway, but I'm not much on mixed drinks). "What y'all got to drink there?" she asked. A "purple rain" they tell her, just tell the bar tender you want a "purple rain". So, she gets one and lets us all try it. It was pretty good too, for a mixed drink, like I said I'm not a huge fan. Michelle and the group were all well acquainted with the purple rain by the time we left Mr. Sancho's, however.

At breakfast the next morning on the ship, we learned all about the consequences of the purple rain. A "purple rainstorm" if you will.

Lisa and I are enjoying our coffee outside on the deck after watching the sunrise, and here comes Michelle. The first words out of her mouth, not a "hey", "how are ya", "kiss my ass", or nothing. She greets us with a...

"What color was your sh!t this morning??"

"What??" Lisa and I ask with blank faces, because honestly this kind of question does not surprise us when it comes to Michelle.

This woman who calmly and peacefully lit a candle in reverence not 4 days ago, just good-morning-ed me with a "what color was your sh!t".

"What color was your sh!t??... Mine was like a lime green!! That can't be normal?? I have never had lime green sh!t before."

I'm watching my big sister, looking for guidance on what to do with this information.

"Do you think it may have something to do with all those purple rains you threw down your trap yesterday?" she asked sarcastically.

"Hmm...I guess I did have quite a few of those. But they were so good!" she says with a roar of laughter. When Kris walks up she gets the same bombardment of questions with not a care in the world who overheard...

"Kris! What color was your sh!t this morning??"

Caribbean color lessons by Michelle: purple goes in... lime green comes out!

Other than the lime green fiasco in the bathrooms, it had been a great trip! Sand, sun, blue waters, shopping, and friends, that are basically family, all make for a near perfect trip.

We were blessed to have one more fun day while on this ship. As I've mentioned before, I'm a nerd, there is evidence of that all over these pages.

I love trivia when on a cruise. The ships always offer multiple trivia games during sea days, in a variety of categories. Christmas, Harry Potter, music, Star Wars, art, sports, history, you name it. I make it a point to go to almost all of them, even if I have to go by myself. These trivia games aren't just for fun! You get a trophy if you win, a very cheap, very coveted, "ship on a stick". In all my travels – I have yet to win one.

There is always one final trivia game onboard near the end of the cruise. An epic battle of wits, that almost always turns into a party. On our last day onboard, there was one more trivia game. The big one! An 80s music guess the song, sing-along, trivia game. Hosted by the cruise director herself, *"Jess from the U.S."*. Since the three older ones in the group grew up on 80s music, and Megan and I listened to it from being around them our entire lives, we were all very familiar with these hits! *This is our chance* I thought, I've got my team, we know all the 80s songs, no one has had any "purple rain", we are going to win!

Song after song we were punching out the answers! Song title and singer! We knew them all! *Guns and Roses, Michael Jackson, Prince, Billy Idol* between the five of us we had it in the bag! Last song comes up and it's the epitome of 80s music. The piano starts, that first note was all we needed, within one second, we start singing immediately...

We scream it out in unison! "DON'T STOP BELIEVING BY JOURNEY!!"

Giving us a perfect score and a "ship on a stick"! Finally winning our first trivia game! We even got a second "ship on a stick" for being the most enthusiastic team!

What a great trip!

Chapter 14
The Forgotten Cruise

Kind of a strange title I know. How do you forget a cruise? Forgetting comes two-fold in this story.

We remember the cruise, kind of. It was fun, it was full of sunshine and sand, and great way to spend another Christmas. Can I tell you anything specific that happened on the ship? Nope. Can I tell you what adventures we went on at the ports? Nope. Even after a recent discussion with Brenden, he told me he couldn't remember one thing we did during that cruise.

The most memorable part of the cruise, when a few of us, no names yet, forgot an entire event at the port. The cruise wasn't the most memorable part of the trip. The two days after we got back... were, however.

The Christmas present of 2017 was you guessed it, another Caribbean cruise. This year was a repeat for me and Lisa, we were going on the same trip to Cozumel and Progreso, Mexico. But this time we would be doing the round trip from Mobile, Alabama.

Mobile is easy enough to get to from our hometown. Like the drive to New Orleans, the time it takes and the mundaneness of the drive, make the trips very similar. You veer off I-55, just after crossing the Arkansas line and take the bypass around Memphis, sticking you on to Highway 45. Don't worry, you spend the majority of the drive in good ol' Mississippi, mile after boring mile. At least this time the drive is on the eastern part of the state, so you don't have to look at the same pine trees and rolling hills as the last trip, you get to look at new trees and new rolling hills.

This trip was a bit of a change up from the others. Instead of arriving in Mobile the day before the cruise and checking the sights out, we got there the day of the cruise and would stay a couple days after the ship returned to check it out. Those last couple days spent in Mobile are a core memory of any vacation I have ever taken and was definitely the highlight of this trip.

The most memorable, or only real memorable part of the cruise happened in the Port of Progreso. As I have said in my previous details of visiting Progreso, it's not the most exciting place to visit. To have fun at the Port of Progreso, you must leave the Port of Progreso.

After the trip, of doing whatever it was we choose to do, we spend a few hours in the actual port. A small gathering of shops and locals selling anything from prescription drugs to hammocks, knockoff sunnies and purses, and every other souvenir you could possibly need. Yes, need. Souvenirs are a need.

Not ready to board the ship just yet, we moseyed our way around the different buildings, making deals and buying random things, we found the Doug sitting on some benches holding the shopping bags from all his girls, enjoying a *cerveza*. Apparently, he found a stand selling said *cervezas* for only one American dollar.

While we continued to shop, Lisa joined The Doug and waited patiently by the dollar beer man the entire time we were picking out our trinkets.

THE FORGOTTEN CRUISE

We started to head back to the ship. In the most random encounters, The Doug makes a friend on our walk back. This random Mexican fella had a homemade walking stick that The Doug was fascinated with. It was a quick friendship, it lasted only the walk back to the boarding dock, but the Doug was so invested in this new friendship, he asked Lisa to take a picture of him and his new friend with a walking stick. Now, The Doug is not exactly a people person per say. To put it frankly – The Doug doesn't like people, so we all were more than slightly surprised as he requested this picture, even more so when he buddied up to him holding the guys walking stick with one arm and the other draped around the strangers' shoulders, like they were long lost besties. Anyway, she gladly obliged. We then boarded our ship, never to see this fella again.

Now what on earth does this have to do with the forgotten cruise? Well, let me tell you.

Later, after we boarded, and dropped off our things we all headed up to the Lido deck for some buffet lunch/dinner. Getting on the ship is always a random time frame, sometimes too late to be considered lunch, too early for dinner, and everyone is way too hungry to wait for said dinner time. So, we just grab some buffet food now and we'll get some "tensies" later at the 24-hour pizza station.

While at our lunch-dinner, Lisa gets out her camera, wanting to show off the pictures she took while in Progreso with her new Nikon. We were all crowded around her, checking out the photos of different buildings and beach life, when she happens upon a picture of The Doug, holding a walking stick, giant smile, buddied up to a Mexican that no one knew the name of.

"Who is that?"

"Doug's Mexican friend with the walking stick." One of the kids' answers, looking at her in stunned in confusion.

Doug now leaning in to get a better view, "My what??"

"Well, who took that picture?" she asks, tilting the camera towards the Doug.

The five of us, Issy, myself, Em, Brenden, and the 10-year-old, are dumbfounded. We all start looking at each other in awe of what my sister just asked. *Is this for real?* In unison we answer her "uh.... You did?!?!"

"No Kidding?? ... Huh, I take a pretty good picture!"

The whole table bust out laughing! They BOTH had zero recollection of this event.

Apparently, she visited the dollar *cerveza* man as many times as The Doug, because she had absolutely no clue she took the picture of her husband with the walking-stick man, and he had no idea who the walking-stick man was.

Wow.

Their children were so proud.

Our cruise ends and we dock back in Mobile. A little sunburnt but ready to see what Alabama has to offer. We only had about two days and nights to spend in the city, the third day would be reserved for traveling.

After getting back to the hotel and unpacking in our new temporary residence, we head out to the cars in search of something to do. It was nearing the afternoon, so we decided we'd grab some grub and then head to the *USS Alabama* Battleship Memorial Park. Featuring a retired war ship from the 1940s, the *USS Alabama*, a retired submarine, the *USS Drum*, and a host of other military aircrafts and land vehicles.

This place is amazing. It is a big kid's playground.

On your drive into the park, you are met with massive artillery machines, tanks, aircraft, along with various transportation used by the US Coast Guard. Tucked away from the road a way but should absolutely not be missed is a set of stone granite pillars honoring each branch of the US Military for the Korean War. Army. Marines. Navy. Air Force. Coast Guard. A massive stone slab honoring each of the men and women aboard the *USS*

THE FORGOTTEN CRUISE

Alabama that never returned from the Vietnam War also meets you as you make your way into the park.

Inside the building at *USS Alabama* Battleship Memorial Park, you have a chance to see many different aircraft and other military mementos. Multiple modern jets are inside this building proving how little space is needed on a war ship to store the multitude of aircraft they carry. Numerous Jeeps and other land vehicles, including a Red Cross vehicle, also inside are helicopters and other retired fighter jets. Numerous signs explain the impact certain groups had on the war, such as The Tuskegee Airmen and Women of the War, and what military park would be complete without The Stars and Stripes draped in dramatic fashion for all to see when viewing these incredible machines.

After we took a looksie inside we made our way out to the *USS Drum* first, saving the best for last in the *USS Alabama*. Are you aware how small a sub is? I was certainly unaware of the actual size of a submarine when we climbed aboard to check out its interworking's. I am 5'2' (5'3" with shoes on) and I felt tall in this ship. Mind you, I didn't have any trouble making my way through the various "doors" that were the size of a porthole. The remainder of my family with all the short jokes did however. I was actually worried Brenden wouldn't be able to get though some of the openings, he had to squeeze through in ways that only a teenager could. Being the short one finally paid off in this case, I guess I missed my calling as a Submariner. Just kidding, I'm not going to pretend to be even close to as brave or as fierce as any military person, the only thing I got going for me is the ability to not have to duck through the openings of a sub.

The *USS Alabama* is hard to miss. This giant made of steel, stands out from the flat waters of the Mobile Bay. Massive cannons and ship guns are seen on-guard in the front and rear of the ship...forgive me the aft and bow of the ship. Huge anchors, which seem minuscule compared to the ship as a whole, will make you curious how they could ever keep something so monumental from drifting. Even after just debarking on a luxury cruise liner, you can't help but be in awe by this enormous ship.

I mentioned this park was like a big kid's playground. That's because you can actually climb aboard the *USS Alabama* like the *USS Drum*. The park gives you the freedom of exploring many of the rooms and different compartments of the ship. From the mess hall to the bunks to the different living quarters of the higher ranked officers, doctor and dentists' offices and even an on-board store made to look like it did when it was a functional ship.

We had a blast checking out every nook and cranny we could on this ship. We had fun "manning the guns", pretending we had the strength to lift even a fraction of the chains that laid on deck, and of course grabbing the photo ops to show the size comparison a human body had to anything on ship. We climbed the tower of the massive ship and got a great view of the deck of the ship along with sun starting to set on Mobile.

We all had a great time here and recommend this for everyone. The girls we could tell were a bit bored and ready to go by the time we headed back to the hotel. Lisa and The Doug enjoyed the experience more. Not that they are military or history buffs but as older adults they can appreciate a rare and unique experience, especially one that honors our bravest. (by older adults I mean older than me, I did not call you old!) I think Brenden and I loved it more than anyone. We definitely felt like kids at a playground, we did not want to leave. We explored every inch we could and wanted to explore more. Like everyone else though, we had to obey the hours of operation. It was one of the neatest things I've ever gotten to explore and would do it again, no hesitation.

On our second full day, we catered to the younger girls a little more. We slept in, ate pizza, a little shopping and headed for the trampoline park. This day's park was more for the younger girls, but I had a blast and of course,

I will forever act younger than I actually am, whether my body wants me too or not. Brenden did too, mostly terrorizing his sisters and me at every chance he got.

We got back to the hotel after a fun day of trying not to pee our pants on the many different trampolines, we still had plenty of daylight and hours left in Mobile. Brenden, Lisa, and I were ready to conquer more of the gulf side city. The girls, however, were not. They had just spent 5 days aboard the cruise ship, with no Wi-Fi, and no service, then two days of running around town. They were ready to text friends, watch Netflix, and check their socials as young teenagers do.

That left us three in a pickle, they were too young to stay by themselves, but not wanting/willing to go out with us. Generously, The Doug volunteered to stay at the hotel with the girls and we were free to go check out more sites. Whether he did that for our sake or his, we're not sure. We can say he was taking one for the team though. Thankful he did because in comes the most fun, exciting, and random thing that has ever happened to us on a vacation.

That evening we left our hotel, in search of something fun to do. We felt a little awkward, it wasn't very often that we set out just the three of us for an adventure. We tossed around a few ideas while heading toward the Mobile River area of downtown. At Brenden's suggestion, we decided to go back to the *USS Alabama*, told you I'd go back again! We spent another evening, checking out the massive ship, skipping the other attractions at the park and going straight for the big one. We explored a few things we had the day before and diving even deeper into the belly of the ship. There is so much to see, we weren't bored at all doing another round in the maze of this battleship.

We once again closed down the park. Deciding we needed to check out the historical area of downtown, we parked and walked the streets like the seasoned tourists we were. The best way to explore is a good stroll around the block, get real up close and personal. Being a coastal town, with just as much history, it brought back memories of walking the sidewalks of New Orleans and Charleston.

We had no real agenda. We made our way in and out of various shops along the street, not buying anything until we get to the old-timey looking candy shop. Full of chocolate covered everything, we couldn't help ourselves here and each got a treat.

While walking these said streets, we happened to notice a growing police presence, but not in an alarming way, just happened to notice a few more police standing at corner streets, chatting and surveying the busy streets that are now getting fuller and fuller with every store we visit.

After a while we notice, not only more of a police presence and a growing crowd along the sidewalks, there is now volunteers putting up those metal barricades along the streets. You know the ones, large gate looking pieces used for crowd control at major events.

We asked the woman bagging up our chocolate treats, if something big was going on, tonight or in the morning, since all the barricades were going up.

"Oh yes!" she exclaimed. "The parade starts in an hour or so!"

"Parade??"

"Yeah, don't you know? The Dollar General Bowl is tomorrow. They are having a parade for the teams and the town tonight!"

A parade!? Heck yeah! We all three look at each other in question of whether we are staying or not, and we all confirmed without words. We were definitely staying for The Dollar General Bowl Parade! We drop off our chocolate at the Jeep and go find our place for a view of the parade.

Did we plan on seeing a parade while on our Christmas vacation? Absolutely not.

Did we have one of the best times in the history of our Christmas Vacations? You better believe it.

I'm from small town America. We know parades! We've discussed how small my hometown is. The county I live in has about 5 "major" towns in it (I am giggling at that sentence, none of these towns are major, one doesn't even have a stoplight). Each one of those has at least one parade throughout the year, if not more. Every major holiday, school homecoming, and even the start of little league baseball. We love parades! This, however, was unlike any parade we've ever seen at home.

It's go time. The line starts coming our way down the street. Just like any parade, there are a few emergency vehicles to lead the way, flashing their lights and occasional bump of the siren. Following that is of course some old cars, maybe a few convertibles, and some carrying the Grand Marshal of the parade or possibly the Dollar General Bowl big wigs. So far it was just like our hometown parades. Then we are met with the biggest most impressive floats. Giant trains; floats in the shape of boats, the size of actual boats; one built as a huge Jester face taking up the whole street. It was unreal.

This parade we went to was unlike any I had ever seen! It was Mardi Gras, Christmas, and Football Homecoming parades all rolled into one and then magnified tenfold. The floats were massive, made of more than your run of the mill papier-mâché. These enormous floats had multiple levels, some even double decked, working lights, places for characters dressed up in their best joker or jester outfits to walk around throwing a variety of prizes to the crowds.

It lasted forever. Marching bands from both Appalachian State and Toledo hyped the crowd with each note they played and chant for their respected schools they would initiate. Trains of multiple connected floats went by. Music blared and crowds cheered. People from all over filled the sidewalks, shouting, singing and having a blast. Some were there to support the teams, some locals, some like us just there on vacation. Float riders threw out everything you could imagine to the crowds. Candy, beads; in traditional green, purple, and yellow, souvenir cups, moon pies, glow bracelets and necklaces, light up swords, fake cigars, little soccer balls, you name it! We were on a drugless high!

This was one of the most bizarre nights I had ever had. All we wanted was to go check out the downtown area of somewhere new and we were met with a massive party. Mardi Gras style. The most random events we have ever experienced.

You don't always need a plan. We certainly had zero plans of doing any of this when we decided to leave the hotel that night. Get out, go with the flow. You have no idea what parade you might run into. Something that will forever be the best memory of that vacation.

I tend to forget the fact that we went on a cruise that year. The carnival that happened in those city streets that night forever will be the highlight of my visit to Mobile.

When we got back to our hotel that night, necks adorned with a multitude of colored beads, souvenir cups in hand overflowing with candy, moon pies coming out of our pockets, wrists covered with glow bracelets and fake cigars hanging from our mouths, we were met with three very confused teenage girls and one dumbfounded grown man.

We told them all about the most random adventure we had just had. Ever since then, those three girls have not once chosen to stay at the hotel instead of going to explore the places we are in.

Chapter 15
Central Colorado

Well, it's 2018. The moment our family has been anxiously awaiting/dreading. My buddy has graduated high school and is now about to start a whole new adventure at college, getting a degree and playing football for the MWSU Griffons.

With that new shift in life comes a new adventure for us all... A graduation vacation!

The grads choice – mountains!!

Lots of them!

Lisa found a great spot near Colorado Springs the summer of 2018. We were going to have 7 wonderful days enjoying mountain air, adventuring, and spending time with Brenden before he headed off to school.

We made the painstakingly long drive through all of Missouri and all of Kansas before entering The Centennial State. I have told you all about how boring the drive from Missouri to the Gulf Coast is, with too many hours spent rolling along Mississippi with nothing to look at but pines and asphalt. Interstate 70 is worse. Way worse.

Joke was on us though as for the next six years and counting, we would be learning every turn of I-70 through Missouri, going back and forth visiting Brenden, and now Em, at college.

Kansas wasn't so bad. At first. With rolling farmlands. Full of beautiful green and yellow fields, contrasted perfectly with a bright blue sky. It was a nice change from our usual drives. However, from Missouri to Colorado I-70 stretches 422 miles. 422! On the same highway, looking at the same thing! Fields and sky! That's it! Even worse, gas stations are spread out like four leaf clovers, you may only see one every thousand miles. That's what it felt like anyway as we pushed my poor Jeep to its max looking for a place to pee. My mother, who I believe was an Indy driver in a past life, had the petal through the floor looking for anything. A gas station, a rest stop, an old abandon house, we didn't care we HAD to go!

Other than the monotony, the drive to and from was fairly decent. We decide to break up the drive there with an overnight stay in Junction City, Kansas. Around six and a half hours of drive time from home that put us pretty close to halfway.

I think my poor brother-in-law had been driving for too long by the time we found a hotel though...

"Hey, what do you think M.T.A. stands for?" he asked the girls this, looking around for some sort of name to go with M.T.A. while Lisa checked us into the hotel.

"What? What are you talking about?"

"Right there on the door. M.T.A. What do you think that means? It's not the name of the hotel."

My sister ever so gently puts him out his misery. "Well, dumbass..." she says quietly so Mom can't hear, "it stands for A.T.M. and you are looking at it from the inside of the door."

Yeah, we all were getting tired, and maybe hangry.

The drive through Colorado was as beautiful as expected. Snow lightly blanketed the peaks as we got closer to the Rockies. When your normal scenic views are nothing but luscious green rolling hills, the massive rock formations rising into the sky above are mind-blowing. Like seeing a cruise ship for the first time or the second tallest skyscraper in America, no matter how big you think it is, it's bigger in real life. It was a definite contrast of scenery from our usual trips.

We were staying in Florissant, about 45 minutes from Colorado Springs, in a massive and beautiful cabin named Dominic's Bear Den. With two floors and a basement level, it was perfect for our group of eight. What attracted Lisa most when she picked this place was the straight shot view of Pikes Peak, the secluded area we were in, and of course the hot tub.

We, of course, check out the entire area as soon as we arrive. Going through every room, the balcony, the back deck where the hot tub and fire pit were located and even around the yard and surrounding wooded area. The sweet folks that rented the cabin to us even left us a care package, candy for the kiddos, and a local coffee mug with their favorite coffee for the adults. Something I wish I would have thought to do, bring them one from Missouri. Hopefully we get a chance to go back one day.

We went exploring the woods and back yard, dotted with mostly pine trees, checking out how different the terrain was from home. Picking a few pinecones off the ground, giving them a good sniff, enjoying the fresh sent and sending my allergies in a spiral.

While on our nature walk, we happened across some bones. Now I need to explain something about my mother. She is the most graceful and kind person you will ever meet. She is also a huge fibber. I don't want to call her a liar, because as my Grandpa Pete would say "it's only a lie if it hurts someone." So, Mom isn't a liar, she just is very creative and wants everyone to have a good laugh, her fibs are never hurtful, they are just Mom being Mom. Well, when we found the bones on our walk, my lovely "creative" mother decided to go Archaeologist on us. She gave us a very elaborate story of how these bones ended up here in this back yard. Stating that this was a mammal, indigenous to the area, from the looks of it most likely a deer or an elk. She explained how it had died, when it had died, and how long it took to decompose. She came up with the most detailed story of this possible deer's life. This could have been a dead dog that was drug here by a mountain lion for all she knew, but that didn't stop her. It may have been a strange thing to make up a story about, but it is something none of us has forgotten. Six years later and we all still tease Mom about her "archaeology days".

The cabin has three levels. Brenden and I took the basement level. Lisa and The Doug called dibs on the master bed on the first floor, and the girls plus Mom took the second floor.

We live relatively close to sea level, when compared to Colorado. Bonne Terre sits sub 900 feet of elevation. Moms new home of Grand Rivers sits even less at 420 feet. Our new home away from home is over 8,000! It's not that noticeable on the drive in, how high in elevation you are getting. It's always said the air is thinner the higher you go. I knew that, but so far, I had not felt any different, breathing in the mountain air was easy and refreshing. Relaxing even. That is until I tried to run up the stairs from unpacking my stuff...

I finished unloading the suitcase, turned off the light, sprinted up the stairs just encase there is a boogie-man in the dark basement and sprint. Reach the landing and...

I. Could. Not. Breathe.

Not even kidding, I had to lay down when I got to the first floor of the cabin. Sucking wind like I had just tried to race against Bolt!

I'm lying in the floor...dying from lack of oxygen, and my whole family is just gazing in wondermont, curious of what on earth was wrong with me. That's fine guys, don't help, I'm good!

What was that!? I work out. I go to the gym on a semi-regular basis. I even run 5k's from time to time, and here I am about to have a coronary from going up one flight of steps!?

When they say the air is thinner the higher you go, they don't just mean at the peak of a fourteener. It will be a very subtle change, but it will be noticed when you are at the top of the steps begging for one more molecule of oxygen to get absorbed in your lungs. Lesson learned the hard way, but lesson learned.

About halfway through our stay Lisa noticed our Mom would stop midway up to the second floor and would make a comment about something.

"Look how pretty the sky is!" pointing out the huge bay windows.

"I really like the décor they have in here." Motioning toward the typical mountain lodge style of décor that was not, in any way, overly exciting.

"I know you just told me, but what are we doing tomorrow so I know what to wear?"

Every time she went upstairs, she had a question or comment about midway up. Finally, Lisa realized what Mom was doing. She would pause halfway up the stairs trying to catch a breather from the altitude, but she would make it look like she just had a question or a random thought.

She got away with it too, for about three days.

The fun is in no short supply in Colorado, adventures are abundant. With rivers, gorges, mountain peaks, and other natural wonders all around how could anyone not enjoy their time here. How anyone can leave unscathed is also a mystery. I mean I have scars just from going up a flight of stairs too fast.

From near heart attacks while ascending 10,000 feet, to almost a man overboard, and near death in a "sanctuary", it's a wonder why any of our extended family still trusts us to travel. If any of these stories prove anything, it's that guardian angels do in fact exist because we've had a lot of "almosts", those poor guys must be very tired at the end of our trips.

We made it through our first few adventures with no drama. A few small steps in the right direction toward maturity when it comes to vacationing... learning how to have danger free fun.

We stopped at the Olympic Training Center in Colorado Springs on our only real rainy day. A massive compound for our U.S. Olympic athletes to train at a high altitude, to help better prepare for competing against the best in the world. A multitude of sports train here, with state-of-the-art equipment. Nothing but the best for our athletes, and this place makes a show of it. Boxing rings, pools, and the epic weightlifting facilities were just a few of the areas we got to visit. A massive countdown was visible for everyone present to see as well, athletes and visitors alike.

Days till Beijing: 1,337

A number that can have a myriad of meanings. A number symbolizing another opportunity to bring home gold, no fear, just readiness for the veteran athletes set to take on another Olympic Games. A countdown to someone's first games, anxious excitement building at a chance to prove themselves. Also, it could be a number of total excitement for us spectators, who watch from the edge of our seats every two years, cheering on complete strangers like they are our own family. Some of these athletes you've grown to know and love watching compete, whether in the sports you've grown up playing yourself (i.e. softball or swimming), or a sport that piques your interest because it is so foreign to you (i.e. gymnastics or curling).

The facilities were immaculate, and nothing disastrous happened while we were there. Nothing totally exciting happened either, every corner I turned I was looking for Michael Phelps. Not once did I spot him out on in the complex training. Not swimming, not running, not lifting weights. Didn't he know the games were right around the corner!?

Nevertheless, my unsuccessful attempt to stalk the most decorated Olympian aside, the training center was worth a visit. If sports are an interest, you'll definitely want to put it on the list.

Another one of our less dramatic adventures was to the Royal Gorge. A massive canyon cut out by the Arkansas River. Over 1,200 feet deep and 300 feet wide in parts, this giant gash in the earth is quite the sight!

To those who are a bit leery of those numbers, don't fret. The gorge has plenty of options for taking in its beauty, some way more adventurous than the others. A massive zip line will sling you all the way across the massive opening. A gondola, that will cart you gently across. Or go at your own pace and walk along America's highest suspension bridge.

We decided on the gondola over and zip-lining back for our round trip. The gondola was neat. Very chill, lazily carrying its load of folks across the massive expanse with plenty of windows to look down toward the Arkansas River.

When you make it across, however you choose, it's not just an out and back trip. There are plenty of opportunities for photo ops. From the bridge to the overlook, plenty of places to take in the incredible creation and get a selfie or two. Another attraction on the other side of the gorge is the Skycoaster. We've all seen them, the massive pendulum swing that you strap into, get pulled upward and then ceremoniously dropped like a bad habit from a heart stopping height.

This "swing" was situated right up next to the edge of this huge whole in the ground known as the Royal Gorge. Well, Mad Dog decided she wanted to do this. All 9 years and 55lbs of her wanted to ride this yoyo made of steel right over the edge of this cliff, to get a real bird's eye view of the Arkansas River.

The guy at the counter promptly told her no, she was too small.

Thank God.

Unless... an adult rode with her.

Crap.

Papa-nope. Mama Lisa-absolutely not. Grandma Teresa-no way.

That left me. I am not afraid of heights. I am not afraid of roller coasters. I am, however, very cautious of giant swings and even larger canyon cliffs. I could just envision myself being catapulted off the side of this cliff to my certain death.

The trip was going so well, I decided it wasn't time to tempt fate.

We skipped the Skycoaster. Sorry, not sorry, Mad Dog.

Due to the amount of wind that day, unfortunately we also had to skip the zip line. The folks in charge of the zip line were afraid that with Mad Dog's small size and the wind amount she would get stuck in the center of the line. They weren't going to let her ride. So, we decided, all or nothing, either the whole family could zip line or none of us would. We opted for the suspension bridge instead. Much to Emily's relief I believe.

It all worked out though, we found a different company to go zip-lining with, though not across the gorge it was equally thrilling and beautiful views. To Em's delight she was allowed to skip this fun. Still not hip on the idea of riding a steel cable across the landscape from thrilling heights, her and The Doug hung back. We had a great time, even with the dry air and altitude making it more of a workout than just a fun adventure. We had a blast, we're hoping one day Em will branch out and give zip lines a try.

Mad Dog also made the proclamation that when she got old enough to get a job, it was definitely going to be a zip line instructor job.

Whatever you say kid.

We saw, met, and nearly witnessed a massacre of our fair share of wildlife on this trip. Rams on Pike's Peak, elk throughout the many fields along the highways, but more importantly we saw, whitetail deer, one of which became like a member of the family, wolves, and one single solitary cat.

Mentioned earlier, our cabin was out away from town, tucked back away from the highway. We had other homes around but nothing too close. So, the wildlife had plenty of room to roam around the neighborhood, around yards and forest lines in the area. We had a group of whitetail deer that would come up to our back deck almost every day.

One little guy in particular became very fond of us. I'm sure it had everything to do with our friendly demeanors and welcoming atmosphere we created around our new home and absolutely nothing to do with the six extra waffles we shared after breakfast one day. Our new deer friend, now appropriately named Waffles, came to check to see what breakfast items we had left each day after that. With no hesitation he would come right up to the back door, letting us feed him by hand.

That was the PG episode of our wildlife encounter.

Out next visit was to an awesome place not far from our cabin. We had no plans to visit here but after passing it on our way back and forth into the city, Em and Issy did some research and suggested we stop and check it out. It was worth it!

This place was The Colorado Wolf and Wildlife Center. A non-profit sanctuary for wolves and other animals alike. You can take tours and learn about the wolves themselves but also about conservation and the challenges other endangered species have.

There is a small gift shop where you can get information about the sanctuary, purchase tour tickets, and get a couple souvenirs to take home. I definitely had to get a sticker for the bestie Katie. She has this slight obsession with wolves, even her twitter handle was @drunkwolfgirl for a time.

We picked the standard tour for our group, but there are plenty of tours to pick from. Feeding tours, Full Moon tours, and interactive tours to name a few.

Wolves with fur of all colors reside here in this haven. White, black, some with a mix of browns, grays and tan. They were all so beautiful and majestic looking. Curious of who had come to visit today, they would pace around the fence line getting a good look. Some were calm and relaxed laying in the shaded areas, lazily picking up their heads to see what was walking past.

Until...

Remember that one single solitary cat I mentioned.

Well, you wanna see a pack of very relaxed, almost friendly looking wolves turn into the predators they are? Have Garfield walk by their cage. Close enough to see and smell, but too far to reach. It was game on. These majestic dogs turned almost scary but in a fascinating way. This poor cat, whether a stray or someone's sick joke I'm not sure, was just meandering around the sanctuary. Every wolf was on edge. Hair standing straight up on their backs, heads hunched over not looking away for a second. Not moving a single muscle. The deep guttural growl slowly rising out of their throats when this cat moved nearby. Stalking patiently and fiercely. It was a fantastic kind of scary.

The entire group was on pins and needles with anticipation of getting way more of a show than we had originally paid for. There was an option for a feeding tour, but we all were about to get that as an unexpected bonus part of our "standard tour".

This ridiculous cat had no fear though. Whether stupid or just really brave, who knows. It somehow managed to get inside one of the wolf cages. Brenden is giddy with excitement over getting to watch the hunt that is about to happen. Some little girl in the group is halfway to a panic attack because Hello Kitty is about to be a wolfie's afternoon snack. I can't look away, the tour guide is trying to lead us on, but no one wants to go just yet.

The wolves will not let this cat out of their sight, watching, waiting for it to get just a slight bit closer for them to pounce.

Somehow, this cat does its typical cat thing and skates out of the wolf cage untouched. All nine lives still intact. I'm not sure who was more disappointed about the anticlimactic hunt, or non-hunt I should say, the tour group or the wolves.

Our next day was major adventure time. Whitewater rafting! Guys, I cannot tell you enough how fun this is.

We picked a company called Noah's Ark Whitewater Rafting and Adventure Company. Located in Buena Vista, Colorado it was about an hour away but definitely worth the drive. We drove through some very wide open and scenic views of Colorado before getting to the start of this adventure. Giant mountains topped with just enough snow was the backdrop for the whole drive. Views, that to this day, I still can't get over.

Whitewater rafting is by far one of the most thrilling, adrenaline inducing adventures I have ever done. Noah's Ark full day tour was almost five hours of the best views of Browns Canyon, right from the water. I cannot recommend this company enough, granted my experience with any other company, up to this point, is nonexistent but they made this trip unforgettable. We all loved this place so much if we ever do travel back this direction, we for sure will be heading out with them again.

We floated on two rafts. Each with its own guide doing most of the work with the oars. The guides sat in the center of the raft with one person at each corner. Brenden and I in the back, Mom and Mad Dog in the front of our raft. In the other raft it was Issy and Doug in the back, Lisa and Em in the front. We were all given a helmet, life jacket, and oar, though the guides did most of the work when it came to paddling. We were floating in June, but the water was still on the chilly side, so we all opted for the "dry jackets" that were offered.

All set and ready, in our matching blue whitewater outfits, we push off into the Arkansas River and down through Browns Canyon. The nervous excitement building with every corner we turned in this river. We were promised a full day of Class III to III+ rapids, with fun little names like Pinball, Zoom Flume, and Raft Ripper, we couldn't wait for this river to show off!

Show off it did! We got our first taste of a rapid, small, not enough to even worry about, but just enough to break the ice. Our guides gave us instructions through the first set of small rapids, shouting out commands for us to follow. Good practice for when we hit the money shot rapids.

"Back 3" paddle backwards three times.

"Forward 2" paddle forward twice.

"Left side 4" folks on the left side of the raft, give her four.

After the practice run, and the instructions mastered, we were ready. We get to our first real rapid, the hearts are pumping and the adrenaline is maxed! Giant walls of water surging through the boulder lined riverbank, crashing against one another creating a maze of current. The raft is rolling, dipping, and rising with every wave, we are at its mercy. It is the most exhilarating experience I've ever had.

Water cascades down small waterfall like drops, maybe a few feet. We roll right with it, gliding through, water crashing over the sides of the boat. The river sprays us with every rapid we meet, like it needs to touch us to make us feel welcome. Rapid after rapid, wave after wave, drop after drop, we are having the time of our lives. Laughing at the sheer thrill of what we were doing. How on earth is this much fun even allowed!

Our guides were the absolute best! They made us feel so welcome and had the patience of saints because all those instructions we "mastered"; they were thrown out the window the first set of big rapids we hit. The excitement was just too much, who can listen to paddling instructions when I've got a wall of water hitting our raft from every angle. They were well prepared for that though, they took charge on all the rapids, got us unstuck from a few spots, and made sure our rafts stayed upright the entire trip. They made us laugh and by the end of the trip the guides we had felt like old friends.

They also have my gratitude because I believe one may have saved Mom's life.

We are rolling through these rapids, in consecutive order, one after the other. Our raft is being bounced around by massive amounts of water. Rock cliffs flank us on both sides, giant stone boulders and massive pines lie on the water's edge creating a great jumble of obstacles for the Arkansas to go through, creating all of this fun. We hit a massive wave, our raft rises straight up and it's like slow motion. I watch as my Mom starts heading toward the water, her body thrown sideways from the crash of the raft against water, she can't right herself. She is going overboard in a Class III+ rapid. We aren't even halfway through the rush of water. She can swim, no problem, but can anyone swim in a Class III+ rapid, if they've never done it before? More like just try to stay above water and hope for the best.

Suddenly, like some kind of ninja, our guide, in one fluid motion drops his oar, reaches out with one hand, grabs the back of mom's life jacket, and flings her back into the raft. He then, without missing a beat, picks up his oar and continues getting us through this booming river. Anything could have happened if she would have gone in the water. But with his skill and knowledge of rafting and of the river, thankfully, we didn't have to find out.

We were given an album of photos after our trip. Dozens of pictures of us in our rafts taking on these massive rapids and the Arkansas River. Dozens of photos of pure joy! This adventure could not have been better. So much enjoyment, so much adrenaline. All in nature, enjoying the water and God's beautiful creation, with some excitement thrown in, naturally.

So please! If you ever get the opportunity to whitewater raft, do it! Don't let fear keep you from doing it. Yes, it does have its dangers, but do your research, find a reputable company, and just give it a try. Start small if you have to. Do a half day float or one of the smaller floats if available. It is a wonderful adrenaline rush full of excitement and memories. Plus, it is a chance to see sights from a different angle. I'm sure Browns Canyon is beautiful from the banks, but it's even more beautiful from the middle of the river, holding on for dear life. Trust me!

Our last big adventure for this trip was a voyage up to Pikes Peak. This monstrosity stands over 14,000 feet above sea level. Only a few miles from Colorado Springs, it's a short drive from the city to the base of the mountain. The drive up takes a lot longer.

There are a few options to ascend this beast. Car, shuttle, cog train, or if you are really crazy, hike. I couldn't even make it up a flight of stairs. I can't imagine hiking 14,000 feet without dying.

Being peak season, we choose to avoid having a timed entry to drive the entire road up to the summit and opted for the shuttle busses waiting just beyond the Glen Cove Visitor Center to help us finish our drive.

The Pikes Peak Toll Road is around 19 miles in total, full of steep climbs and switchbacks galore. Beautiful scenes are visible throughout this whole drive as you make your way around tight corners, up and above the clouds. Pine and aspen forests, smaller peaks of the Rockies, the breathtaking vastness that Colorado has to offer viewable from every window.

Also, visible just out your side windows is a nauseatingly steep drop off, mere inches from your car. Every switchback required a dangerously close drive near the edge of this road. At some points we were headed up and around at such an unnatural angle, so steep I had to lean over the steering wheel just to get a view of the road.

To give you some perspective on how steep this ear popping drive is, on the drive back down the mountain, there are checkpoints you have to stop at so someone can check the temperature of your brakes. If your brakes are too hot, they have a potential to fail and send you careening off the mountain at what I would assume a very uncomfortable rate, and almost certain death. So, if your brakes are at an acceptable temperature, you may pass, if it is not you are required to pull over and let the brakes cool off before you are allowed to proceed. It was one of the more stressful drives I have ever taken in my life.

A lot of that had to do with my mother yelling at me from the front seat of the Jeep. If I so much as looked in any direction other than toward the road, even for just a split second to take in the views. I would hear *"AMBER! YOU HAVE GOT TO PAY ATTENTION!!!"*. Which is real rich coming from the woman whose hands follow her eyes whenever she is behind the wheel. It's a little difficult to enjoy the view when *"AMBER!!"* comes at you when you do. But I did my best to appease my mother. Keeping my eyes toward the road and the car between the lines, getting us to the shuttle busses in one piece, and not to the bottom of the mountain in record time, like she imagined.

The other vehicle in our convoy didn't fare any better. My sister, lover of all things high up, was white knuckling the "ocean handle" the entire drive with one hand, slapping The Doug in the arm with the other between every word she yelled toward him.

"Douglas!" slap.

"Pay!" slap.

"Attention!" slap.

In her defense, this was the man who made a complete random exit on the way to Colorado, for no apparent reason, other than he "thought" that was the way to go, even though Google never gave him those instructions, and we had never been there before to have those said "thoughts".

He did however, with the patience of a saint, sit in the driver's seat, taking all of the slaps and panicked yells about being too close to the edge or too close to the guard rails or going too fast. Saying "yes dear" and proceeding around each switchback as gently as possible to keep Lisa from losing her marbles before we even got to the good views. She did apologize for freaking out once we got to the top.

Once at the summit of Pikes Peak, you are greeted with a 360° panoramic view of the beautiful and majestic Rockies. Above the clouds you can grab literal breathtaking pictures at 14,000+ feet of the incredible landscape that surrounds you. If you are lucky enough like we were, you can be welcomed to the summit with a gentle snow! I was prepared for colder temperatures the higher we got in elevation, however with-it being June I wasn't expecting to get snowed on. It was a very welcome surprise.

A visitor center, of course, graces the top of this summit. With a wide selection of t-shirts, coffee mugs, keychains and every other item you can think of with "Pikes Peak" stamped across it, it's good enough reason to stop in. The main reason you need to make a stop in this visitor center, however, isn't the souvenirs. The reason may be a little surprising, it's a rite of passage if you will, but don't leave Pikes Peak without stopping in for.... Donuts!

That's right. Donuts.

This beautiful building pops out over 6,000 donuts a day. Like cheese curds in Wisconsin, Gooey Butter cake in St. Louis, or deep dish in Chicago, Pike's Peak Donuts are a staple! This is the only place in the world where one can consume donuts made at 14,000 feet above sea level. Due to the elevation, the process to make these wonderful fluffy circles of sugary goodness, is much different than at a lower elevation. If you were to try to take some home for later, you would be severely disappointed, because they would no longer be fluffy delight, they would most likely resemble a donut that has been run over by a car.

As we were about to leave, Emily decided maybe she did want to try the high-altitude donuts and ran over to get some before we headed out to the bus.

And this is where my beautiful niece, simultaneously made the cashier feel like a weirdo and herself a complete doofus!

Cashier: "So where are you guys from?"

Em: "No thank you!"

Now confused cashier: "Oh, uh ok."

Em walks back toward us, then stops dead in her tracks with realization. "OH MY GOSH! He asked where I was from not if I wanted my receipt!!"

Be sure to pop your ears at the top folks, that way you can hear better and can avoid awkward conversations like this one.

I guess we should have mentioned that to Em.

We unloaded the vehicles of vacation gear after a very long trek back. Then had to almost immediately start filling it with things to make Brenden feel more at home in his new dorm. Move-in day was approaching.

The adventure mishaps didn't end when we got home that summer. We drove over 1,800 miles that round trip. A few days after we got home, we got some very shocking news from The Doug.

"You know how we just drove across three states and back?" he chuckles with an exhale of breath. "Well, we didn't have insurance on the truck that whole time.... Or for the past three months!"

"WHAT!?!?!?" Lisa shrieks. "We went all that way without insurance!?"

"Yeah... but just think of all the money we saved..."

Chapter 16
Southern Caribbean Cruise 2.0

After walking through the thick jungle, the large Belizean man turns around to face us.

"Who's ready for a snack?" he asks, no emotion on his face. The humid tropic air is causing sweat to drip off his temples. His question is met with very little excitement from the group, also dripping with sweat, they were deep in the jungle after all. Neither accepting nor denying his invitation at a little treat as they muttered a response. Most were already banking on the red beans and rice dinner that awaited them after the "main event".

"Well…" the Belizean says, taking a small insect from a nearby tree, "here it is…" and ceremoniously downs the tiny six-legged creature. This got more than mutters from the group. A few gasps, a couple of "oh gross", and more than one "ewwwww".

Christmas vacation 2018 was set to be our biggest Christmas trip yet. We once again planned a Christmas cruise in the Caribbean. This year however we were scratching two more countries off our list, Honduras and Belize, while also making two stops in Mexico. This year we were venturing farther from home than we had ever been. Setting sail on the *Carnival Dream* for seven days of fun and adventure in Mesoamerica.

We made our favorite drive ever, I-55 toward New Orleans. No issues arise this road trip only the expected boredom through Mississippi. We discussed the adventures we were going to try, what the two new countries were going to be like, and what the possible crazy things that could happen this year.

With a bit of research beforehand, we narrowed our itinerary in Honduras down a week before we had set sail. Cozumel's excursion was also a given, we were going back to Mr. Sancho's. The only stops we hadn't locked down an adventure for... Costa Maya, Mexico and Belize City, Belize.

We are a group that likes to do our "research". As soon as we know where we are going, sometimes alone or sometimes together, we will look up all options of adventure for our stops. *What does the cruise ship offer? What has the most reviews? What are other people trying? What makes this place unique?* Google, Google Maps, TripAdvisor, Facebook, Pinterest, there are so many places to find information these days on what fun there is to have. I personally am a map person. You could hand me a map of where we are going (i.e. Google Maps), or heck a map of my hometown, and it could keep me occupied for ... a while. That's how I like to look things up for my trips. But the options don't end there. You can get personal with it, ask workers on the cruise ship, join a Facebook group dedicated to that certain area, if at a resort -ask the front desk service. Remember do your research! Don't just pick the first option that's offered to you. Make sure it feels right.

So, after a bit of research looking at the suggested adventures from the Carnival website, Emily desperately wanted to go cave tubing in Belize. The kid was growing up and really starting to branch out. She no longer had the stubborn teenage approach to trying new things, "if not my idea I don't wanna". Her desire for adventure was kicking in, thankfully the midnight float on "The Saint" hadn't scared her away from that. She found this adventure as something new and exciting that we would all enjoy, and she was right. It didn't take a lot of convincing to get the remainder of the team on board.

One small problem though. The cave tubing trips themselves were deep in the heart of Belize. A one to two-hour bus ride would be required to get to the caves. I'm all about booking with locals when it comes to excursions, but two hours one way was putting us at too much risk for missing the ships onboard time. The only compromise, we would have to book through Carnival. Problem with that was the only cave tubing excursion offered was a "cave tubing and zipline adventure". Going that deep in the Belize jungle, we either did them both or neither, which meant no cave tubing. Which was fine for everyone, but the planner herself. Emily was branching out in adventure but still wasn't keen on riding a giant steel cable hundreds of feet in the air, but she so badly wanted to cave tube. So, she decided to "man up". Our Belize adventure was set. Jungle zip-lining and cave tubing.

Our first stop on this Christmas adventure, was in Costa Maya, Mexico. Located also on the Yucatán Peninsula, but further south than our recent ventures in Progreso and Cozumel. Since we had already planned out our adventures in the other three ports, we decided to wing it here. We also decided to go easy at this port, opting for a simple beach day.

When we stepped on the dock we were greeted with the usual crowds. Other travelers from our ship and other ships at the dock, plus numerous tour guides and cab drivers waiting to take us to explore their beautiful coastal town. We found a booth selling tours and simply told them what we were looking for, and with no hesitation they pointed us in the right direction.

We were taken to a semi-private beach by bus charter only a few minutes away. With plenty of beach, ocean views, drinks, and souvenirs galore, we were in for a nice relaxing day at the beach.

Though not all inclusive and definitely not the most beautiful beach we had ever been too, it was a great day. We rented kayaks and took our first attempt at kayaking in the ocean. With calm and shallow waters, we had no troubles paddling the Caribbean waters here. Plus, we had had a lot of practice by now on how to handle rough waters in a kayak, so we were well equipped to handle, or at least try whatever the coastal waters had to test us with.

On just about any beach, you can almost guarantee the locals are going to make their presence known and sell you whatever they can. Parasailing, pictures with a parrot, henna tattoos, braids in your hair, and so many other possibilities. That was all spot-on here too. Normally, I/we will give them a smile and a no thanks and they go on their merry way. This trip however, a group was coming around asking if anyone was interested in snorkeling with sea turtles. Em, Issy, and I were very interested in this tour. We had never seen sea turtles outside of an aquarium. So, after some discussion with Lisa, she gave us the okay. (Yes me too, I may be an adult but sometimes my sisters approval is still needed. I've had to get her approval more often than I have from my Mom or Dad.)

After unsuccessfully trying to convince her to come with us, we headed out to swim with sea turtles. Remember earlier when I said do your research? Well, I'm about to give you an example of why. Also, an example of possibly one of the dumbest things I have done in Mexico.

Em, Issy and I, start walking with our tour guide, toward the boat that will take us on our adventure. Except we don't walk toward the boat dock that is in sight of where our beach chairs are set up, no, no, no, we walk probably a half a mile down the city street by the coast to another boat dock down the beach. I assumed we would be going over to the nearest boat dock, so I went barefooted. Well, I was wrong. This entire walk was uncomfortable, physically due to my raw feet and chaffed legs from walking while still wet and sandy. I also felt very uneasy about walking with these two teenagers I was now responsible for. We were heading off on a boat with a group of Mexican tour guides that we had *just* signed up for an adventure with. Yeah. Dumb. The guides were nice, and seemed very knowledgeable about the ocean and the wildlife. However, this responsibility was new territory for me, I felt uneasiness to say the least.

This is now what I consider the dumbest thing I have ever done in Mexico. My intrusive thoughts had me reconsidering the idea the entire walk to the boat. I was thinking about every bad thing that could happen. The older me now is also cursing myself for the potential danger I put my two nieces in. I don't think I ever mentioned this to any of my family, but I can't believe we actually did that.

I was questioning our decision even more when we got to the boat. Not a complete piece of junk but it definitely wouldn't be my go-to ocean cruiser. We went out on the boat, me thinking the whole time, *why did I not just say never mind and take the girls back to the beach*. I did start to feel slightly better when our tour boat started heading back the direction we had walked from, toward the beach and the remainder of our family.

Like our sailboat with dolphins excursion in Florida, technically this trip was a success as well. We did see the sea turtles and a few other marine life. More importantly we did not end up on the evening news for going missing in Mexico. It was, however, a bit of a disappointment, and probably not what you would imagine. There were not swarms of sea turtles surrounding us, nor did we ever even get close enough to get a good picture. Our tour guide was quick to point out when one was near, mostly because our chances of noticing the sea turtles on our own were very slim. The calm waters that we had kayaked in were now long gone and choppy waters had now replaced them, making it difficult to not to suck water down your snorkel.

The boat returned us to our family, safe and sound, near where they were lounging. No more raw feet from the walk back. It was an experience, and I guess a successful one. But not one I'd like to ever be repeated. My fears may have been unnecessary but that isn't always the case. So, I will say, if something feels uncomfortable, there is probably a reason for it. Do your research when planning an adventure, make sure you get a good one, you don't want to remember your trip for the wrong reason.

Lisa and I returned to Costa Maya a little bit later on another girl's trip with our work family. This time our excursion was a way more enjoyable experience. On this particular trip, we booked a private beach a few weeks in advance. Someone had seen it on Pinterest, (like I said, lots of places to do your research), at Maya Chan Beach Resort. Which is an all-inclusive day resort, by reservation only.

Food, drinks, hammocks, beach games, and pools. This was just the place we needed to relax and have fun. We couldn't swim in the ocean that day due to some unfortunate water conditions, it was something the owners forewarned us of and offered to give us a full refund, should we choose not to stay. That was unnecessary, we didn't have to be in the ocean, all we needed was the sun, a cold drink, and to not be at work.

The food was incredible. We watched the very practiced Hispanic woman behind the counter as she chopped fresh ingredients for our Pico de Gallo; seared up delicious steak, chicken, and fish, for tacos; and patted out her homemade flour tortillas with ease. The food was so amazing, I even tried the fresh ceviche. A dish that I had tried before and was not at all a fan of, but the way this woman had prepared everything else with love and skill, I thought I'd give it a try. It was just as amazing as all the other dishes offered.

Among the amazing homemade food, they also had house made tequila. I am not a hard liquor drinker I am a complete wimp and quite frankly I don't like the taste or the burn, but when in Rome, right? Or in this case, when in Mexico. I was very surprised to find there was no burn, it was smooth as could be. They didn't offer it for sale to take home, if they did that would have been the only time I would have considered it.

I tell you this in hopes that you'll add it to the list of options should you ever take a trip this way. My first time around Costa Maya was assuredly not my favorite port of call, but after this little gem of a beach resort I have changed my stance. Like Mr. Sancho's in Cozumel, Maya Chan will be a must stop when visiting this port.

The second stop we made on this trip of adventure was in Mahogany Bay, Honduras. Situated on the largest of the Bay Islands of Honduras, named Roatán. Honduras has been in the news a lot lately I am aware, and not for heartwarming reasons I know. This trip to Honduras, however, was nothing short of fantastic. No danger, no fuss, and we had planned our trip ahead of time and picked out the best excursion.

On a recommendation from a friend, Lisa booked us an all-day adventure at a private island hotel, named the Little French Key. It is a little island off of the main island off of the mainland, of Honduras. Only so many folks are allowed, which means no crowds. Little French Key was just that, no crowds, you couldn't even accidentally wander into this place, because you had to have a boat to get here.

The resort was beautiful and quite unique. As soon as you stepped off the "shuttle boat", you were met face to face with a jaguar, the mammal not the car. Caged of course, its menacing teeth met us with a mere yawn at our arrival. No more bothered by us than the group of chimps housed nearby.

We walked around the boardwalk guarded by the tropical trees dipping low, toward the beach area. The greenery opens up and we are met with one of the most beautiful shades of blue water I had ever seen. Protected by a coastal barrier, this little cove of water was sparkling blue and as calm as could be.

This resort had a little bit of everything for everyone. There were classic beach loungers and bar, for the more relaxed group. There were giant swings to sway on or to get a few tropical pictures while perched on. They offered hair braiding, which all three girls took part in. There also was tropical animals that I've mentioned. More exciting are the water activities. Everywhere you looked were beautiful clear waters to swim and snorkel in, a massive platform that you could jump from, or better yet take the rope swing off of, with a stomach dropping height straight into the crystal waters. Another new venture for us we tried and loved, was paddleboarding. A perfect spot to test out the balance as well, with the calm protected waters, we tried and failed multiple attempts to get onto these extra-long surfboards. All of us except the youngest that is. With her petite child body and low center of gravity, she was able to climb aboard and immediately stand up. She ended up paddling circles around us as we struggled to even get on the boards without falling off. After a few attempts we all got our "sea legs" and loved our new water sport.

Honduras may not be at the top of everyone's bucket list, but I couldn't recommend where we were enough. The people were friendly, and it felt very safe. We even had a great time just talking to our cab driver on the way back to port. The water was beautiful and the adventure was plenty.

We make it to Belize on our third stop. We are hungry for more adventure. Em's thrilling excursion is just hours away. No backing out now. Eager as we were, we wouldn't have dreamed her idea of adventure would get us this much excitement. With a new experience waiting for us in "The Jewel of Central America", we head to the gangway as soon as possible.

Like The Cayman Islands, cruise ships are not allowed to dock close to land. Instead, you take "tender" boats to and from your cruise ship to the port. Being on a schedule, we hurriedly got ready, grabbed a snack and went to where the line started to board the tender boats. Boarding the boats is not usually a hard task, the crew directs you what to do and when, and as long as you put just a little trust in them, and yourself, it is not a difficult job. As you are standing in line watching the hordes of other folks, young and old, trying to judge the roll of the small boat alongside the cruise ship, looking like a very timid child with every attempt, you'll start second guessing your decision to get off the ship.

We make it across the bay in our tender boat into Belize City. I know I preach about booking tours with locals, but this time booking our tour directly through the cruise ship did give us a bit of ease as we boarded our bus. Knowing that no matter what happened in that jungle we were headed to, the ship would not leave without us. By the looks of this bus, car trouble was high on the list of possibilities.

No worries though, the almost two-hour bus ride went without issue. It was hot, a much-welcomed temperature for a few Midwesterners in December. There was plenty of scenery to gaze at through the windows. Driving through, what one could only describe as the countryside, we passed through mostly farmlands. Rows and rows of orange groves, corn, and other tropical staples. Deeper and deeper into the heart of Belize until we finally made it to the Caves Branch River.

We prepared for the first leg of our adventure, packed our valuables away in the provided lockers, and received instructions on how to don our zip-lining harnesses. Everyone had a general idea on how they were to fit, except Emily that is. This would be her first zip-lining adventure. She wasn't keen on this part of the trip but if she was nervous, she didn't show it. A benefit of her stubbornness. While waiting for the remainder of the group to harness up, we were encountered by an amazing aroma. Something savory, with just a hint of sweetness. Chicken, red beans, and rice with plantains, were simmering nearby. Something the guide promised would be waiting for us after we finished our full adventure, and it would be worth the wait.

We made our way through the thick jungle toward our first zip line, looking like a row of troops with the host of others that had also signed up for this adventure. Single file up the trail, ascending the man made, yet made to look natural, steps. We take in all the flora around us, comparing these beautiful tropical plants to those we have in the Midwest. They don't compare in case you were wondering. We hook on to our first line, excited for the thrill of another adventure in a far-off country.

Lisa, ever motherly, is watching Em like a hawk. Gently reassuring her it will be fun. Though she never let her nervousness show outwardly to us, a mother always knows. One after another we whiz down the steel cable through the massive palms and overhanging branches, getting a random glimpse at how far up we actually were. The buzz of the pulley on the cable and the rush of wind, it really is a thrilling experience, even if you've done it before. We all land on the platform with a jolt of the harness against the stopper. Em giving us the "that's not so bad" nod of approval, we all head off to the next platforms. Some now more willing than before.

After the thrill of zipping through the dense jungle, we head back to the locker area to trade our zip-lining helmets and harnesses for caving helmets, a headlamp, and a river tube. Getting to the caves required a short jaunt through the jungle, but on a well-worn path. This was obviously a very popular excursion, for good reason.

It is here that our tour guide offered us a "snack". With a playful yet serious invitation, he offers us a tasty snack of fresh.... Termite. That's right, the six-legged creature he plucked from the tree and then chomped down on was a termite. He was now inviting us to join him in his snack time treat. What?!?

I have tried some unique foods. Gator, escargot, spam, liver, raw fish, pickled okra, fried conch fritters, just to name a few. I will try anything once. But a termite?? One that is still alive until you munch down on it?? That sounded a little too wild for even me.

Mr. Belizean Bear Grylls proceeds to grab another one and thrust his hand out to the group. "C'mon they taste like mint!" as it crawls around on his finger in attempt to escape.

Hold up. You mean to tell me this bug that's barely the size of a grain of rice has a taste, and not only a taste but a taste that is actually considered refreshing?? I'm thinking all of this to myself with dumbfounded look on my face, staring at this big man's hand with a tiny termite darting around on it looking for an exit sign.

Brenden and I start quizzically looking back and forth between this tour guide and each other. Both now with a smirk, as if to say, I'll do it if you do. Curiosity got the best of us.

We both agree that if you want to be adventurers, then you have to be adventurous. We both took a termite from the guide, and yes, we were the only ones, said bottoms up and stuck them in our mouths. With the tiny physique of the little things, it required a very delicate and precise first bite. Wouldn't you know it, with that very small crunch, a burst of mint blanketed our tastebuds! It was not a horrible experience like you might would imagine. Of all the "unique foods" I listed above that I've tried; it doesn't even rank near the bottom.

The cave tubing was a thrill. Not quite the river adventures we've had in the past, but it was its own unique adventure. With nothing lighting the way except the lamps on our helmets, we weaved our way, perched on our inner tubes, throughout the darkened cave. Echoes of our voices off of the tunnels of rock, the sound of rushing waters fill our ears. Small waterfalls inside the caves surprise us with each blast of water they welcome us with. Laughter fills the cool cave as we make trains of people on our tubes, squeezing around each corner. It was a fun and a rare experience that we were all glad Em found it for us. And yes, the lunch that we were promised would be worth the wait... definitely was.

But of course, we couldn't end without an almost disaster.

Back at the docks to board the tenders that will ferry us over to our ship, we did a little shopping. Souvenirs, tee shirts, and lots of jewelry stores lined the streets at the port area. We notice the wind picking up and our bright and shiny day is now starting to get really dark, really quick. So, we make our final purchases and head to the tender boat line. By this time the wind is gusting, and the dark clouds are rolling in, a storm is on the way. Nothing to be alarmed about, it's the Caribbean, it rains every day. Now it's our turn to board the tender boats that are rocking and bobbing with every wave crashing the dock. I had to really watch my step when boarding, following the motion of the tender with my raised foot so not to miss. The Doug boards, he helps the girls board, Brenden boards, I board, then when it's Lisa's turn to get on, the dock hand says they are shutting the tender boats down till after the storm passes, this is the last one, and then proceeds to pull the gate closed!

"Woah, woah, woah!!!" Brenden, Doug, and I start shouting almost in unison. The girls are alarmed. All of us thinking that Lisa is going to get left in Belize, alone, without her family. Being stranded in the Caribbean, what a shame, I know. But with all our uproar over the dockhand closing the gate in front of Lisa, the tender boat captain said to let her on. No splitting up the family.

She's slightly annoyed, curious about what an adventure it would have been to be left in Belize. But she boards and a sigh of relief escapes our mouths. Sorry sister, you must stay with the fam!

Our fourth and final stop on this wonderful Christmas getaway is to a place we are all now familiar with. Cozumel, Mexico.

We opted for our favorite, a beach day at Mr. Sancho's. It was easy and a good deal. Blow-up slides and trampolines in the water, snorkeling, all-inclusive food and drink, pools and hammocks to lounge in. What more could you ask for, for $68?

This day for me is slightly embarrassing, but in the spirit of transparency I'll tell you about it anyway. Remember as we were leaving Belize a storm started rolling in? That storm turned the Caribbean into a beach goers ruin. The wind was still gusting the next day, the waves were massive and persistent.

We got to Mr. Sancho's that morning, they informed us that the beach was closed, no swimming, no snorkeling, no blow-up slides. Total bummer. Oh well, we thought, we still have all you can eat and drink, multiple pools, and plentiful sunshine! And in the end, we still aren't at work, how bad of a day can it really be?

Apparently, not a bad day at all, when you've sat at the swim up bar for hours and hours. With the magic wristband that will get you anything you want. With no way to burn off the excess alcohol running through my 5'2" body (5'3" with shoes on), my inexperience was showing.

Not in a bad way. I am just extra eager to share...or so I've been informed. I just wanted to share my stuff. My coconut shrimp, my money, my coconut shrimp, my thoughts, my coconut shrimp, my extra towel, my coconut shrimp...

From what my lovely nieces and nephew love to bring up, I offered each of them some of my coconut shrimp no less than ten times.... Each. If we ever get to reminiscing about Mexico, one of them insists on bringing up the coconut shrimp fiasco. Oh my, if I were to order coconut shrimp at another restaurant, I'd never hear the end of it. I don't see what the big deal was, I was just trying to share!

As I was laying in my bunk that night, waves crashing against the ship so hard I thought a pirate ship had to be lobbing cannon balls at us. The storm still wreaking havoc on the Caribbean Sea, I couldn't help but be grateful, headache aside, that we had survived another trip and another set of "almosts" to add to our collection of vacation mishaps.

Every time I recall what has happened on our trips, I always wonder ... could they possibly get any crazier??

Chapter 17
The Last Cruise

C ould our trips get any crazier??

That was what I said.

You know, you should never ask questions like that. I fully believe God has a sense of humor and will answer those questions, and probably not like you were expecting.

Christmas of 2019 was the last year of the Christmas cruise vacation. With COVID shutting down the entire world three months after this trip, we are no longer able to adventure for Christmas for the foreseeable future. Back to boring ol' present under the tree for the time being.

This year was a repeat-ish of a previous cruise. A 7-night Western Caribbean trip, out of New Orleans with stops in Mexico, Grand Cayman, and Jamaica. This differed slightly from our previous 7-night Western Caribbean Cruise. Instead of Ocho Rios, Jamaica we were porting in Montego Bay, instead of the *Carnival Dream* we would be sailing on the *Carnival Glory* and lastly Mom would finally be rejoining us on our adventures! After a three-year hiatus, she finally decided to buck up and try another cruise. We assured her, that the waters in the Gulf were way calmer than the waters in the Atlantic. Probably no need for a vomit buckets this time around.

Probably.

A week before the trip starts, I hurt my back at the gym. This was the first time I had hurt my back, and I had no idea what damage I had actually done. I wasn't ready to deal with it seriously quite yet, so, I just asked my doc to give me some meds to ease the pain enough to get me through my trip. Unbeknownst to me, the Doug had also done the same thing and was also walking around like an old man. Trip hadn't even started, and we were two backs down.

We left out of NOLA again, stopping in Cape Girardeau to pick up Mom, well more like she picked us up. Her Challenger can get us places a lot faster than the ol' Jeep. Even with the cracker box sized back seat, it was much more comfortable than the Jeep and bonus I didn't have to drive.

The drive was as boring as usual when heading down I-55. That is until we were about halfway between Jackson and New Orleans. The current driver of the Challenger had a bathroom emergency that needed remedied. Immediately. We are flying down the interstate. I've mentioned Mississippi doesn't have a lot of options at times for bathrooms. The emergency is getting more emergent and that's when we noticed The Doug is no longer behind us.

I get a phone call at about that time from Lisa.

"Hey, do you have any water in that car? We had to pull over the truck is overheating!" Well crap, that's not good. We are already a handful of miles ahead of them by now, with an emergency of our own a'brewing. I knew Mom always kept a case of water in the trunk for "emergencies" though this probably wasn't what she had in mind. I look to the driver while on the phone and say "yeah… do you want us to turn around?"

The current driver looks at me with absolute dread. We head back at the next exit. Sweat now dripping from the driver's face. We find where Lisa and Doug had to pull over and come up behind them. Dousing the engine with some water, it gets back to a normal temp, and we can head on our way. The driver of our car making sure the others had extra water, so we didn't have to come rescue them again. Now we are speeding toward the nearest bathroom at record speed.

When you gotta go, you gotta go.

This trip was starting off very interesting. With more than one type of pain hitting us on the drive down, this was shaping up to be an adventure for sure.

Our first stop on this grand adventure was to Montego Bay, Jamaica. We chose to go a little different adventure this time. A little more laid back if you will. We didn't book this in advance and we kind of waited till the last minute, so there weren't a lot of options for us as a family of eight. But what we chose, turned out to be fun for everyone.

It started off with a bus trip around part of Jamaica on our way to one of the oldest plantations on the island. Here we were given plenty of time to explore the main house. A beautiful 1700s plantation, that was kept in immaculate condition for all to enjoy. Bright tropical flowers met you around every corner, and the windows of the home look out among the hilly Jamaican forest.

After we got our fill of the historical aspect of the grounds we were taken to the more exciting addition to the grounds. A collection of pools, grace the plantation grounds near the Martha Brae River for everyone to enjoy on a muggy tropical day. A giant rock waterfall sits along one of the pools, that you are welcome to climb and take a plunge into the water from. Sitting atop the wall is a waterslide, that of course, everyone took part in, not just the kids in the group. Curious about how this would feel on my stiff and injured lumbar, I asked the friendly staff manning the slide if it was a bumpy way down? In the classic cool Caribbean accent, he reassures me I had nothing to worry about

"Nah, mama, no worries....'id smooth sailin' go'en down"

Our last bit of adventure, included in this tour, was more for the Doug. A rum tasting for those over 21. The four of us did try them, since it was included in the tour. We were given a little taste of 3 Jamaican made rums to try. The rum tasting wasn't my favorite, but I believe the Doug had fun. It was pretty convenient of Carnival to offer a tour that had something for everyone at one price. Historical plantation, water slides and pool, and rum tasting.

This wasn't probably something we would have picked on a normal day, but with waiting till the last minute it was one of our only options. It turned out to be a pretty good day. A little something for everyone. Nothing dramatic happened, although a Jamaican called me mama, which I can only assume is a term of endearment and not that I look like I was the mother of these four kids following me around.

If a relaxing day is what you crave, this is a great option.

Our next stop was to the beautiful island of Grand Cayman. I was so stoked to be going back here. The island and the waters surrounding it are so stunning. I had really hyped up our stop here to Mom. I couldn't wait for her to see how incredible this place was.

Although I was fully willing to swim with stingrays again, Emily and Issy came up with another great idea. We were going to visit the Cayman Turtle Centre. A wildlife center that focuses on sea turtles and conservation but also has other marine life to see. Tours that include viewing sharks and other predators, the 11' Cayman crocodile, and a hatchery for viewing new turtle hatchlings in the right season. This was a great and unique find the girls made and it was going to be so much fun!

THE LAST CRUISE

Was.

It was going to be.

That is until the Caribbean unleashed its fury once again and a storm had ruined our fun. Not only did we not get to visit the Turtle Centre, but we also didn't even get to go to Grand Cayman Island at all. Since Grand Cayman is a port that requires tendering to the island, and the wind was so bad from the storm that had blown in that night, the port authority was only allowing a couple of ships to anchor. Ours wasn't one of them.

I felt terrible because I had talked this trip and island up to Mom so much and now we wouldn't be going. As usual, she let it roll off, said we'd just have to book another cruise that stopped here again.

With our port day canceled, we used our extra "sea day" to explore the ship. We tried things offered on the ship that we normally didn't try. Lisa and I went to a jewelry sale, not because we wanted to buy any of the thousands of dollars worth of bling, but because they were offering free mimosas to the attendees. We had never tried a mimosa, and today was all about trying new things.

After that we did our typical on-board trivia games, people watched by the pool, double fisted ice cream cones as we walked through the lido deck, and played more trivia. Mom decided she was going to go play bingo with her spare time, so she was off to find that while the kids and I tried to win the Friends trivia. We lost by one. We decided to stay for the movie trivia game. Lisa and the Doug were asleep in lounge chairs by the pool and Mom was off dobbing away at numbered squares hoping for a win. We lost big time at the movie trivia and decided to cut our losses and go find our people.

Doug and Lisa were still snoozing by the pool. So, we went to see how the bingo game was going. We arrive just in time for the final jackpot game and find Mom near the middle of the crowded auditorium. We ask how it's going and of course she's had no luck so far and with only this last game left, things weren't looking good. It looked like a lot of numbers had been called so we decided to wait with Mom till it was over and then all go find something to do.

"B-6"

"O-67"

"I-18"

"Dang grandma you almost have a bingo!" one of the kids said. Now we are all on the edge of our seats! Mom does almost have a bingo!

"G-54"

"Bingo!!!" it comes from a woman across the room. Dang it. So close.

"Wait! I have one too!! BINGO!!" that one comes from Mom! She did get a bingo! With all the excitement of the other lady winning, it took a moment for Mom to realize she also had a bingo. With confirmation from the staff, that was two good bingos! Although they would be splitting the jackpot, neither woman cared! They just won a thousand dollars each while on vacation.

Although the original plan was ruined with the storm, and the fun adventure we had planned was no more, the day ended up being a total success! Mom grabbed her winning bingo card to claim her money and headed toward the gift shops!

Our next day was a port day, and it was about to get real....exciting...

December 20th, 2019, started out like any other day on a cruise for us. Lisa, Mom and I, and sometimes a couple of the kids would all get up early and watch the sunrise from the lido deck while enjoying the strong brewed coffee offered. We did that this day too. Watching our ship sail toward Cozumel Island, ready for another day of adventure at the beach.

After our sunrise and coffee, we all got ready for the day, packed our backpacks with towels, goggles and a change of clothes. After most everyone was set, a few of us decided to go up to the top deck to watch our ship dock. To some this may seem like a boring experience but what else are you going to do? Sit in your stateroom?

That is where this became the most exciting cruise, we had ever been on....

```
"2 Carnival Cruise ships collide in Cozumel,
    Mexico; at least 6 people injured"
  -Gwen Aviles NBC News; December 20, 2019
```

While up on the deck, standing by the railing of the starboard (right) side, we are noticing something different about how this ship is being docked. I had been on a fair amount of cruise ships and almost always get up early enough to watch it being docked. Something about this time felt different. We were turning at a higher rate of speed than I had noticed before, I look toward the other side of the boat and see nothing but sky. *Are we tilting??*

The starboard side is also the side that was facing the land, the dock and the other ships already at port. As we were turning to pull up next to our "parking spot", we are going in at what felt an entirely too fast rate. Anyone who has seen a boat of any kind pull up to a dock knows they go extremely slow, so not to run the boat directly into the dock. We were going too fast. We all knew it. Not only are we headed for the dock at too fast a rate, we are also heading for the other ship already anchored down.

As we all look toward the already moored ship we are about to side swipe, Lisa and I notice many people from the docked ship gathered on their stateroom balconies watching this disaster unfold. Waving at us as we brace for impact against this other ship, like we are a float in a parade passing by. A look of panic settles on a few faces as they, and we realize, this is too close. Way too close!

With quick maneuvering and by the grace of God, we managed to not kill all of these nosey folks on the other ship. We make our way out into deeper waters for another attempt at docking. Whew. That was close!

As we head back around this time, things seem to be going a little smoother. At least I can see a horizon on the other side of the ship and not just sky. Nice and level is better. As we come back around for the second time, we are at a close but safe distance from the other ship, a passenger aboard that ship yells over "That was pretty close, wasn't it?"

We exchanged a few *Yeah that was crazy's* and continued watching the ship pull into port. And then the wind got really strong! Right as we were parallel with the ship that we almost hit the first time, we were now headed dangerously close to them for a second time. I can only assume the person at the helm of this ship realizes once again we are about to slam into another gem in the Carnival fleet, and is desperately trying to pull us away from the dock and the other ship.

We are still at the rail watching our ship start to turn and pull away from the dock again. Suspensefully watching as the stern(back) of our ship, starts coming around toward the bow of the other ship. Questioning, are we going to clear it? Are we going to hit it?

"We are going to hit it...WE ARE GOING TO HIT THAT SHIP!" I keep repeating, almost screaming, to the others around. "There is no way we are going to not hit it!" At about that time, I hear a sickening sound of scraping, grinding, and crunching metal on metal. Like a thousand tin cans being shredded. A screeching, nerve racking sound, that only belongs in car crash scenes in Hollywood.

There was no panic, there was no dramatic jolt of the ship, no alarms going off, people weren't screaming and running around, had we not heard it or been up top, we might not have even known what had happened.

Once again, our ship swings around, third time's a charm, heading toward the dock. Gentler, calmer, more precise. We come parallel to the other Carnival ship, and it is apparent that yes, we did hit the other ship. Giant bruises of damage are evident on the bow of the *Carnival Legend*.

Cuts and marks that only another heavyweight hitter could have made, the *Carnival Glory* that is.

We finally get moored to the dock, and after some time, for what I assume is damage assessment by the crew we are allowed off the ship. On the plus side, our shipwreck gave us a few extra hours to spend in Mexico. As we get off the ship to gaze at the damage ourselves, and the giant hole that used to be one of the formal dining rooms, my mother turns to us with more excitement than I had seen on her face the entire trip. She exclaims "This is just so exciting!!"

The other seven of us roar with laughter and awe. Only she could find excitement in a shipwreck, and declare this to be the most exciting and adventurous part of our trip. She was right though, it was *so exciting!* It for sure was something that we would all remember forever. And much like when we were named the stroller family, "This is so exciting!" took on a life of its own as well. Anything we do, good or bad, will always now be "So exciting!"

The shipwreck did not affect us in the long run. Everyone in our crew was safe. We now had a new and exciting story to tell, we were given a few extra hours in Cozumel to spend at Mr. Sancho's and the souvenir shops. We got to listen to everyone tell their version of the excitement at one point or another.

The trip back to New Orleans was uneventful. The delay in leaving Cozumel did not cause us to be delayed in getting back home. We arrived bright and early the next morning. As we were packing our things to leave the night before, Mom stopped us all, "Wait! Where do I cash out my bingo winnings??"

"Well…Mother" Lisa said with bafflement in her voice "I don't know…. None of us have ever come back with more money than they left with!!"

Can you ever think back to a moment in your life, and think *yeah, that's where things went crazy*. For us it started on this cruise. This was a trip for the books. After a whirlwind of emotions and mishaps on this trip, our lives would be changed even more after we got home. In just a few short months the world would be turned upside down. Fear of illness, like most of us had never seen before, would be blanketing our communities. Loved ones succumbing to this terrible virus. Travels, gatherings, and celebrations would be canceled. Hospital workers suffering in terrible working conditions, physically, mentally, and especially emotionally.

Like many other major events, with images burned in our minds, I remember exactly where I was when it hit our corner of the world. Anxiously awaiting the arrival of my new baby nephew, Briggs. In the waiting room of a local hospital, a member of the staff told us not to leave until after the baby was here and we had gotten to see him, because they were currently placing into effect a no visitor policy for all patients.

Like many of our trips, this was not what anyone had planned for this occasion, but that didn't stop it from being one of the greatest days. Being an aunt is one of the greatest privileges in life.

The next 2-3 years were not what anyone could have planned for either. Like it's always said, "Man Plans, God Laughs". Our Christmas cruise adventures have been suspended for now...

But don't worry, none of that changed our crazy travels, we just had to adjust course....

Chapter 18
Amarillo, TX

In 2020, like many things, football season was canceled. This was foreign territory for everyone, especially in our family. August to November, for the last 17 years, had meant one thing for us. Fall sports season. Now, with everything all messed up, the fall football season would be nixed. By some magical turn of events, the athletics program for MWSU managed to schedule four games for the team to play and families to watch. Only two of which they actually got to play.

Which is where our first trip post COVID comes into play.

Brendens college, MWSU, managed to schedule a football game, farther than the team would ever travel during a normal regular season. They were scheduled to play against West Texas A&M, in Canyon, Texas.

So, Lisa and I took a couple vacation days, bought our game tickets, booked our flights, and reserved a hotel in nearby Amarillo, Texas. This was going to be a great weekend away to a new destination, to relax and watch college football.

That is until...almost the entire coaching staff contracted COVID. Game. Canceled.

After hanging up with Brenden, learning that the game was canceled, and he would be staying in St. Joseph, Lisa calls me. Sounding disappointed she tells me what Brenden said, and with some hesitation she asked, "What do we want to do?"

"Um... I don't know... what do you want to do?" I asked, also hesitant, because I knew what I wanted to do, but was afraid it wasn't what she wanted to do.

"I guess we could probably get our money back on our reservations.... Or..."

"Or??" slightly excited

"Or... I guess we could still go?"

"Yeah! Let's just go anyway!"

We both were on the same page about still wanting to take a long weekend to Amarillo but were unsure how the other would feel about it. We obviously should have known our answers would be "Yes let's go on the trip".

After hanging up with me Lisa goes upstairs to tell her husband, the Doug, about the canceled game. "Huh" he mutters, "guess, you'll be able to get your money back for all your reservations, yeah?". She gently breaks it to him that we weren't even going to try, we were just still going to go on the trip anyway. No football, no problem. We can find something to do, I'm sure.

Our flight took us from St. Louis to Dallas to Amarillo. Medium airport to massive airport to tiny airport. Amarillo by far is one of my favorite airports. There is nothing special about it, no secret layers or anything. It is, however, very small, and fairly new. Other than the airport at St. George, this was the least overwhelmed I've ever felt at an airport. Ironic, because the most stressed I've ever been at an airport was was in St. Louis, for this trip.

I had realized the day before the flight that I hadn't flown on a plane since I was 15. For some reason, known only by God himself, that fact gave me uncontrollable anxiety. Things they don't tell you about turning 30... you get knee crippling anxiety at the dumbest of times. I think Lisa still has nail marks on her arm from my death grip. You'll be glad to know I have gotten over that anxiety in recent years... mostly.

Where is the first stop you make when you leave the airport?

The hotel? Not us, nope, it's dinner!

Our first stop in the great state of Texas- The Big Texan, home of the 72-ounce steak, and the 72-ounce steak challenge.

That's right 72 ounces! That's four and a half pounds of beef! For reference, the average human brain is 46 ounces. That's almost two brains! An NFL football weighs between 14 and 15 ounces, that's five times a football! The kicker... you have to eat it, plus a shrimp cocktail, baked potato, salad, and buttered roll, in an hour!

The 72oz. steak challenge is pretty well known, and had the football team actually made this trip, I'm certain a few would have signed up, and probably won! If you finish you win, if you win, your meal is free. If not well, you have to pay for the entire meal and the 72oz. steak.

Someone was attempting the challenge while we were there, unfortunately they lost. We decided to skip the challenge, but we did eat entirely too much food anyway. Definitely add this to your stops if you are ever this way. Even if you don't try the challenge, it's worth a visit. The food is great, and the atmosphere is too. Plus, you might get to see someone throw up while trying to eat a 72oz. steak!

We hadn't made any plans for when we got to Amarillo. Mostly because football was our main objective while we were here. With that now a no go, we were kind of wingin' it the remainder of the trip. We were only here for two days so we needed to make it count.

We checked out Cadillac Ranch, which apparently, is a big "attraction" in Amarillo. The word ranch may give you the impression it has something to do with farming or animals. No, this "ranch" is a very peculiar... art display. This sculpture garden, if you will, is a display of 10 Cadillacs, buried nose first in the middle of a desolate field.

While this may not seem exciting, it is fun in its own way. While graffiti on a normal day is frowned upon and can even get you in a bit of legal trouble, at Cadillac Ranch it's not only allowed but encouraged! All 10 of these former junkyard staples turned art display now demonstrate an array of neon pinks, lime green, electric blue, gold, sparkly silver, and the classic black. Paying homage to anything from smiley faces to visitor names, to hometowns, these 10 cars are a way for visitors from all over to sign the most unique guest book, in whichever color or signature they so desire.

On the plus side, this little tourist attraction is free. Free to visit, free to take pictures. The only thing that might cost you is a can of spray paint, if you so choose. However, we got very lucky, and a very nice kid gave us his lime green as he was leaving. Left in it was just enough for me to paint a "573" on the side of one of the cars, my way of saying "Hello from Missouri!".

Our first night at the hotel was a lot more eventful than the day's activities. Since we were only staying for two nights, we picked something cheap near town. All we really cared about was, "did it seem safe?" and "did it come with two beds?".

On our first night, after an exhausting day of travel, we chilled in our room after dinner, and went to bed with the old people at 9 p.m. It didn't

AMARILLO, TX

take long for the both of us to fall right to sleep, it had been a long day that had started early. We were ready for a goodnights rest so we could be ready for adventure the next day.

Did we get that much needed rest you ask?? Nope! The alarm clock so conveniently woke us up at 2 a.m.!! Lisa hits the off/snooze button and with a grunt of annoyance, it stops squawking and we turn over to go back to sleep. Or so we thought...

ERRT. ERRT. ERRT.

"What in the actual!?!"

The stupid alarm clock starts blaring again what feels like only minutes later, even though it now reads 2:30 a.m. Lisa now slams her hand on the off/snooze button with a growl of aggravation. Both of us are completely annoyed now and more awake than the first time. I'm wondering why on earth the alarm is set for this early, was it for someone's convenience or was it someone playing some sick prank right before they checked out of the room. I somehow managed to fall back asleep after being woke up twice now when, you guessed it...

ERRT. ERRT. ERRT.

That freaking thing is going off AGAIN!! It is now 3a.m. and I am ticked. Then in one of the funniest moments of my life, I witness my sister turn over with violence in her eyes. In one solid motion she rips the alarm clock off the table and from the wall, plug jolted out of the outlet and throws it against the opposite side of the room. It crashes against the drywall and lands on the floor in a heaping mess.

"Wow..." I say, stunned.

"Bet it doesn't effing do it again!!!" she says and rolls over to go back to sleep.

I do not go back to sleep because I am in tears with laughter. Guess we'll have to try that goodnights rest tomorrow.

With only one full day of exploring the great state of Texas, we knew we wanted to do something in its great outdoors. After doing a bit of research we settled on Palo Duro Canyon State Park, aptly nicknamed the Grand Canyon of Texas. While hiking and nature was on our list of things to do, what really pulled us to this location was a Texas staple, the Texas Longhorn. However, whether it was due to COVID, or this was their norm, the park required reservations, something that is growing more and more popular as park visits everywhere are on the rise. Needless to say, we were unable to secure our spot at Palo Duro Canyon.

That, however, did not stop us from trying anyway, as we played dumb while pulling up to the entrance, telling the guy at the guard stand "oh, we had no idea you needed reservations, sorry". With that fake innocent mistake act, we were able to get our much-wanted peek at the Texas Longhorns from the turnaround at the entrance. So, it wasn't a complete waste of a trip.

No worries. We were able to enjoy the beautiful landscape that Texas had to offer from a different state park. Caprock Canyons State Park to be exact. A beautiful area full of hiking trails and wildlife for all to see. We were not at all disappointed in our change of venue.

To get a full overview of the park, I'd recommend taking the scenic drive, as we did, around the park. It is just enough to give you a glimpse at what the Caprock Canyons has to offer. With plenty of places to stop along the drive, you are met with gorgeous red landscape all around. Jump out of the car at one of the pull-offs, or trail heads to get an up-close look. Rocky formations rise up with multiple red, orange, and brown layers, dotted with the random green of shrubbery of Juniper or other desert plant life. It is unlike any landscape I have ever seen; we definitely weren't in Missouri anymore.

As you drive, you have an opportunity to meet wildlife of the very large and the very small variety. Bison have made this place home for a very long time, and while they don't seem to mind that you are there to visit, they won't go out of their way to make you feel welcome either. Throughout the scenic drive you will find traffic at a standstill, waiting patiently for a herd of the famous Texas Bison to cross the road. Sometimes one lonely bison will make its way down the asphalt with the traffic just to stop to a halt in the middle of the road to look around. Personally, I think the furry beasts are doing it on purpose, keeping themselves entertained.

One of my favorite creatures to gander at while on the drive were the prairie dogs. The way they pop out of the ground like a game of Wack-a-mole is too comical. Tiny little brown bodies will pop from the dirt, look around, with an almost confused look of *how did I get here?* It will certainly entertain anyone.

After adventuring we had amazing dinner at Bracero's Mexican Grill and Bar. A must in my opinion, this was some of the best Mexican food I have ever had. If you are keeping score, the best Mexican so far has come from Mexico, Wisconsin, and now Texas. Which feels like a game of "spot the lie" but it's not.

We head back to our room after dinner and a bit of souvenir shopping to pack and get ready to go home the next day. And to hopefully get that much needed nights rest, since we didn't have much luck the first night.

That much needed rest was put to a screeching halt when at 3 o'clock in the morning, we were both awoken to a terribly high-pitched siren. Accompanied by a strobing white light coming from the upper corner of our room.

FIRE!!

I was so sound asleep I woke up completely dazed and ran to the door of our room and flung it open to see where the danger was. What a real sight I must've been, as I stand there in my underwear and tank top, door wide open, ready for action like I was somehow going to stop this fire half naked.

"Get back in here you idiot!!" was what I heard as I came to my senses a little bit out in the hallway, still half naked. Realizing after I woke up a little more, that there was no real danger. The siren stopped almost as soon as it started but not before the first floor was greeted to a spectacle. So much for sleep on this trip, guess we'll sleep on the plane.

I don't know what was more stressful on this trip, the hotel of no sleep or the travel. After putting out the nonexistent fire I finally fell back asleep. I woke up the next morning, well actually just a couple of hours later, to a message that our first flight would be delayed due to fog. That didn't really bother us though. We were just going home; we didn't care when we got there.

Which was good because, our first flight delay gave us about 14 minutes to get to our connecting flight in Dallas. Everyone around us was frantically trying to will the plane to deboard so they could make their next flight. Lisa and I decided we weren't even going to try, we only had 14 minutes to get off the plane, get on the tram, and make it to the next gate before it left. So, we opted to just change our flight home and have a longer layover. Not ideal but it is what it is.

While waiting to deboard I noticed an elderly couple in the row behind us were very anxious to get off the plane so they could make their connection. I mention to Lisa "We should let these old people go first ahead of us since we are changing our flight." I guess I had made too many old jokes the past couple days because her response...

"If I turn around and these people are 45 years old, I am kicking your...." Well, you get the drift.

We spend our layover at a restaurant by our gate, enjoying the people watching. I find myself much more relaxed for these flights home. Odd considering we've missed one flight and have had little to no sleep. But overall, it was a great trip. It did not go according to plan at all. We didn't get to see any football games, the park we choose to go to wouldn't let us in, our hotel refused to let us get any peace, but I wouldn't change a thing!

Chapter 19
Southern Utah

As the year 2020 wrapped up, the new year, and the "new normal" was here. So, Lisa, Mom, and I decided this year, we ourselves, would start a "new normal". That is, we decided to start taking a trip, a big one, just the three of us, every year. No kids, no husbands, just us. We decided to go really big for our first one. A week adventure in Southern Utah, to see the beautiful Zion National Park.

This trip was unlike any other. It still remains one of my most favorite journeys I've ever taken. The beauty and wonder seen throughout southern Utah is unreal. The colors, the immensity of the land, the new and exciting adventures we took. This trip left a mark on me. I have loved travel since that first cruise I took, but this place changed my love of travel. I realized the splendor that this country has to offer is immeasurable and shouldn't be missed.

We flew into St. George, another small and easy-going airport. While most people opt for staying in the nearby town of Springdale when visiting

Zion, we choose a cabin a bit north of the park in Duck Creek Village. We had looked up the expected temperatures for Zion before packing. We were leaving Missouri and its brisk averages in the 50's and headed toward comfortable 60° to 80°. It was going to be beautiful and warm, something we were really looking forward to.

That is until we realized as we pulled into our cabin driveway, that there is still snow on the ground! Not a lot, but enough to question if we took a wrong turn somewhere. Okay, we say, no worries, maybe it just snowed recently and hadn't melted yet? It'll be fine. That in fact, was not the case. We woke up the next morning early, before the sun even, packed up our backpacks and hiking boots, and headed for the car. WOAH! We are met with a crisp 22°!! We are not packed for that. I think I brought one hoodie, and that was because I wore it to get on the plane in St. Louis.

It turned out fine though, thankfully. I don't do cold well. The elevation of our cabin was almost 5,000 feet higher that the visitor center in the park. So freezing temps to start but absolute perfect weather when we got into Zion.

I've never been to Disney World, but I would imagine the anticipation and the anxious excitement we had driving into Zion was comparable. Southern Utah is beautiful. I know, I'm on repeat, I say that about a lot of places. This was unbelievable. Winding through the east entrance of the park on Zion-Mount Carmel Highway was breathtaking. We hadn't even made it into the park yet.

Coming out the other side of the Zion-Mount Carmel Tunnel, I was speechless. If I had to guess what Heaven looks like, this is definitely one corner of it. Massive rock formations jut up from the earth towering over the river valley below. Making you feel so small and so inspired. "Wow. Wow. Wow." Was all I could say as we traveled around the multiple switchbacks of the highway.

We had 4 days to explore this beautiful area. We decided to "take it easy" the first day, get a lay of the land, see what would interest us most. The visitor center and gift shop was an obvious first stop. I detest the mall, but I will drop a Benjamin at a gift shop so easily.

We choose two hiking trails for the first day, you know, to "take it easy". We ended up hiking a total of five miles for our "easy" day.

The Riverside Walk is at the very end of the Zion Canyon Scenic Drive, which requires taking a shuttle to during peak season. This was a very easy trail, around 2 miles round trip and it was mostly paved, it follows along the Virgin River. A perfect choice for our official first hike of Zion National Park.

Next, we took the shuttle to the Zion Lodge to get to the Emerald Pools Trail. This was a bit more strenuous of a hike but not horrible. Around 3 miles, this trail takes you up toward Heaps Canyon past the three Emerald Pools. Giant cliff faces tower over you at the Upper Emerald, a mist of a waterfall can greet you in some portions of the trail. Beauty was in no short supply here. The splendor of the land made these hikes seem so easy. Every corner we turned we were met with a picturesque view unlike anywhere we had ever been.

After hiking all day, with nothing but Lunchables and peanut butter crackers to snack on, we were hungry. Some of us even teetering into hangry territory. This becomes a big problem throughout this trip. It's Easter weekend, which may be a prime time to visit the National Park, it is not however for the town we are staying in, or even the towns nearby. There is nothing to eat here!

We are starving and can't find a single restaurant that is open for the "season" let alone still open for the day. We are close to panic. It was looking like our only option was driving hours away to a larger city or eating the remainder of our hiking food. I am a fan of the Lunchable, but that is not dinner. After one more Google search for something to eat we found a pizza place still open not far from our cabin. After ordering salads and an appetizer, the waitress asks what kind of pizza we wanted. I said a large "Hot Mama", Lisa said a large "Pig in the Garden", Mom said a large "Hawaiian".

The waitress just stands there staring, "You want 3... Large pizzas? They're pretty big..."

"Yes!" in unison.

We felt very judged at that moment. She was right though, they were very large pizzas, they were also delicious and even better for breakfast the next day... and the next.

Every evening was a game of Where's Waldo, except it wasn't Waldo we were looking for, it was dinner. If you visit Zion, make sure there is somewhere to eat nearby, because your waitress may judge how much pizza you order.

Our second day of hiking, started out much like our first. Early morning, freezing temps as we leave our cabin, perfect temps as we get into the park, and building excitement as we make our way into Zion Canyon. This was going to be our most strenuous day. A hike to Angels Landing.

Well, almost.

We took the shuttle to the trailhead near The Grotto, crossed the Virgin River via the walking bridge, and started the ascent. Switchbacks greet you within your first mile up the trail. A little more prepared for the effects of elevation after our Colorado trip, this first series of rises in the trail wasn't that big of a deal.

We were given warning by a fellow hiker the day before that trekking poles were a must for this trail. So, we gladly went back to the gift shop and spent a few more dollars to make this hike easier. I am so glad we did. Not only was I still enduring the pain of a back injury from 2020, but Mom was also a couple months post-COVID pneumonia and still wasn't back to 100%. The trekking poles came in handy. Especially when we hit the most famous set of switchbacks, known as Walters Wiggles. Twenty-one steep switchbacks you must climb to reach the remainder of the trail. Thankfully, there are plenty of places to stop and rest. Don't let this deter you though, if a 65-year-old post-COVID, and a 32-year-old with a herniated disc can do it, certainly you can too.

We make it to the top of Scout Lookout, and this is where our climb ends. The remainder of the trail to Angels Landing is steep, and very narrow and extremely crowded. Lisa, who has told her fear of heights to *suck it* this entire climb has drawn a line at a knife's blade shaped cliff. Like the 3 Musketeers, we are all for one and one for all, so if she didn't go up, then Mom and I weren't either.

I can hear the haters now; we actually heard the haters then too "I can't believe you came all the way up here and aren't going to do the chain section. What a waste." That was what a very snarky woman told us on the way back down Walters Wiggles.

No, we didn't do the chain section, for our own personal reasons. Don't feel sorry for us though. Scouts Lookout was one of the most spectacular views I've ever taken in. God blessed us with perfect weather to view this perfect land. Bright blue skies backdropped the massive rock forms rising up all around us. A palette of colors so unimaginable I was rendered speechless. Sheer drop-offs on each side to heart-stoppingly gaze over, was an adrenaline rush that I couldn't get enough of. We sat there eating our Lunchables, taking in this breathtaking view, not a care in the world.

Not a care in the world until we realized we had to pee. When on a hike and "nature calls" what do you do… that's right, hold it or pee in the woods. We certainly couldn't hold it; it would take forever to get back to the trailhead. Peeing in the woods wasn't an option, there were hundreds of people around.

Wait… what does that sign say?

Restrooms this way?? All the way up here?? Who would've thought?

Scouts Landing has a restroom at the top. Not only is it conveniently placed at the top and hidden from view, it is the most hysterical restroom I've ever seen in a park, maybe anywhere. Lisa comes out of the bathroom first. She just looks at me and Mom and shakes her head. Both of us unsure what that implied, we gave her a questioning look.

"You'll see." Was all we got in response.

Read carefully- Poop escalator.

This glorified outhouse has a poop escalator! What is that you may ask? Let me explain. You do your "business"- it lands on a 'belt' of sorts- then you pump a foot pedal- the belt moves, and the "business" rides the belt up and away.

Poop Escalator.

While doing some research before our trip, we realize we are about an hour away from another National Park, Bryce Canyon. So, on a whim, we figured we would check it out. Not knowing much about it we weren't overly hyped about going, but almost felt obligated to go since we were so close. Well, we were in for a shocking treat.

Talk about unworldly. This massive canyon will make you feel like you've landed on Mars. Huge Hoodoos rise up like spindles from the earth beneath. Red rock formations of unruly design will surround you on the Queens Garden trail, making anyone feel oh so tiny. Especially when you are only 5'2" (5'3" with shoes on).

After hiking through all the Hoodoos, we dropped another massive amount at the gift shop and checked out the entire Bryce Canyon scenic drive. This random, on a whim, "obligation", turned out to be an amazing side trip. I can't believe we didn't think this would be worth a visit.

So, please, if you are visiting Zion, take the time to visit Bryce. These beautiful brothers of Utah are so spectacular, and neither one should be looked over.

On our second to last night, we had a decision to make. We had one day left of adventuring, what were we going to do? Spend another day at Bryce, because we had no idea what we were getting into? Check out more trails in Zion? Or try another adventure we didn't think was possible?

The Riverside Walk trail ends in the Virgin River. This is where The Narrows trailhead starts. We did not think this trail would be an option, because even though the air outside was in the 70's the water temperature was nowhere near. And hiking The Narrows requires walking through the Virgin River, sometimes waist deep or deeper, the river is the trail. However, when on our first hike on The Riverside Walk, we noticed people in "drysuits". Which are basically bib overalls that don't allow any water in. Hmmm... could it be possible then??

After some debate, we decided we *HAD* to do this. Now knowing it was possible to walk the river and not get hypothermia within the first mile, we were going in. After some research, we found an outfitter right outside the entrance to the park, aptly named Zion Outfitter. We got our suits, our waterproof boots, and our walking sticks (a must), and the outfitter even dropped us off. One of the best decisions we have ever made.

The Narrows is by far one of the absolute musts if you are anywhere near Zion National Park. You will be in absolute shock and amazement by this creation. This beautiful river accompanies you the entire route, sometimes with a swift flow challenging you to keep going. Massive walls of stone flank you, towering above you, this canyon will make you realize how small you really are on this earth. Sometimes the rock towers merge together so close they nearly provoke claustrophobia.

Spectacular, magnificent, breathtaking. None of these words seem to be enough when I think about hiking through The Narrows. Around every turn in the river, you are struck again and again by how amazing this place is. Kids, older folks, rookie hikers, and veteran hikers; people of all kinds were here enjoying this masterpiece. Some showing how tough they were by walking through with just shorts on, some like us, donning all the apparel because we don't handle cold well.

We were even met by a lone whitetail deer that wanted to appreciate how majestic this place was. Don't let the description deter you, the cold water, the current of the river, all are bonuses to this hike. If you feel like you can't handle the entire "trail" don't, we certainly didn't. Just get yourself a little taste, trust me it is way beyond worth it.

People of all sorts have stated to me, on more than one occasion "I can't believe you go on vacation and do all of these adventures with your Mom!" Of course I do. Mom, Lisa, and I, know each other better than anyone. We can be ourselves to the purest form when we are together.

On our last night, as we packed up, ate the last of the 3 large pizzas, and cleaned out the remainder of our hiking snacks, deciding which ones could go on the plane and which would become this night's side dish, we discussed this latest endeavor we were just on. We were in total admiration of God's beautiful earth, stating how blessed we were to get to do something like this. Simply in awe of what an amazing trip we had.

In the still silence of reminiscence and admiration... one burps so loud it fills the whole cabin... one snorts a giant snot rocket...and the other laughs so hard she 'cuts the cheese'...

Like I said we can be ourselves.

"Bunch of ladies you're raising here Mom!" Lisa says with tears falling while we all laugh hysterically.

That my friends is why going on trips with these two is my absolute favorite.

Chapter 20
Blue Ridge Mountains, North Carolina

After our extremely adventurous trip of 2021, (I have never left a vacation more exhausted) we decided to scale back the spring of 2022 for our mother-daughters trip. This year we decided to take a relaxing few days in the Blue Ridge Mountains of North Carolina.

This was a distinctive trip in its own way. COVID was still a thing apparently, so we had to mask in certain places, mostly just the airport. We crossed North Carolina off the list, staying longer than just the drive through. We didn't even have any drama.... Just kidding, of course we had ridiculousness on our trip.

This trip started with me getting into an argument with a certain man in my life before we left. Him saying that I shouldn't be going to North Carolina, and I was definitely not to go hiking while I was there, "they have bears there!!" Yeah, we have those here in Missouri too, I don't really see the problem. Needless to say, that fueled my desire to go even more, my last name is Black, and we don't handle being told what to do well.

Our trip took us into Asheville, through the Pisgah National Forest, and we stayed in Banner Elk, NC. We also took a day trip over into Tennessee and the Cherokee National Forest for some real adventure.

Banner Elk is a great little town. Small, quaint, not overly crazy busy (although we went in the early spring, so that could change depending on the season) and it's within driving distance to a lot of fun places to visit, bonus it has places to eat, unlike where we stayed in Utah.

As stated in previous chapters, what is the first thing to do when getting off the plane? Go find something to eat. Oh man, what we found to eat in Banner Elk. Wow. It didn't matter that it offered more than one restaurant, because we went back to that same place. Over and over. To get one thing!

We make our way into the restaurant Sorrento's Italian Bistro, after the classic "where do you want to eat?" "I don't care, where do you want to eat?", argument. Finally deciding this was easy, right in the middle of town, and who doesn't like Italian?

We walk in and it's white tablecloths. Hmmm.... Did I mention we just got off the plane. I don't know what you wear on a flight, but I am doing my best impersonation of a high school teenage boy, baggy sweats, large tee, crocs with socks.

The waitress that greeted us did not even remotely care though, she was super sweet and welcomed us. Right after talking with her a bit we discovered she was from a town near our hometown. Small world.

Now, what is this delicious meal that brought us back to this one restaurant multiple times on our trip, and still has us craving it to this day??

Artichokes.

Yup, that's it, artichokes. It wasn't even a meal. It was an appetizer. But it was the most amazing appetizer in all the land. Made with lemon, and butter and a white wine sauce that I cannot get over. Please, please if you go anywhere near here, go to Sorrento's.

But let me come with you!

As stated earlier I was told not to go hiking while in North Carolina. So, I found a few hiking trails for us to go on while we were here. We hiked a few that we found along the Blue Ridge Parkway, arguably the area's biggest attraction. Spanning 469 miles, it links The Great Smoky Mountains and Shenandoah National Park. Thus, making the Blue Ridge Parkway a National Parkway, and giving another opportunity for National Park enthusiast to put one more stamp in their books.

The Parkway is a great "activity" in and of itself. It doesn't require a lot of effort to enjoy. Simply get in the car and drive. The road wraps around the mountains weaving and flowing with the land. The path made to fit the mountains, not the other way around. Lookout points litter the over 400 miles of scenic drive, giving you ample chance to take in the amazing views of the Blue Ridge Mountains. I'm not sure what causes it, something very science-y I'm sure, but they really are blue. Give yourself all day to enjoy this, it's worth it.

One of our big hikes we made was at Grandfather Mountain. Home to the mile high swinging bridge and so much more. I was given an "absolutely not" when telling Lisa this was on the agenda for the trip.

Things that are high= No!

Things that are swinging bridges= No!

Things that are both= Absolutely Not!

I was the driver this trip though, so we went anyway. To my surprise she hiked with us up to the mile high swinging bridge and even crossed it with us. Not without a few remarks and barfing sounds but she still went!

The views were amazing, 360° of pure mountain range. It was a clear day too, so the landscape stretched out in front of us unobstructed by clouds.

Don't let the mile high part discourage you, it is not a mile high from the ground, it is a mile above sea level. The views you will get from the top are amazing, even in the early spring when we went, I can only imagine what it would be in the fall. I may have to go find out one day for myself.

Grandfather Mountain also has other charms in is boundaries. A visitor center for one. Yeah, we went; yeah, we spent too much money. Also, a Nature Discovery Center, crazy natural rock formations, wildlife habitats, a grill and picnic areas. The best part for me however was the simplest little sign by the road.

My brother Josh and I will quote movies to each other all the time. We can go days without a real conversation, but no doubt our conversation history in between has multiple random movie quotes. Randomly texting each other some crazy random movie quote with no other context has been a natural thing to us for so long. So as soon as I spotted it, I knew I had to show him this sign. And I got the perfect reply in return... "I just felt like runnin'"

On a complete whim, we came up with an idea for our last full day in the Banner Elk part of our trip. "Let's go whitewater rafting" one of us declared. So that's what we did! This is where our trip ventured over into Tennessee, and where for once in our life we got to witness family vacation drama and not *BE* family vacation drama.

We went with Wahoo Adventures in Erwin, Tenn. The Nolichucky River was a beauty. Winding through the dense forest of both the Pisgah and Cherokee National Forest, we got to see the splendor of what both states had to offer.

Our group included two rafts, Lisa, Mom and I in one, with a guide of course. A mother and younger daughter in the other with their guide. That family had left their matriarch in the car at the outfitters home base, she wasn't allowed to adventure like ours was I guess. (don't worry, they cracked a window) Our mother would never allow such things.

The rafting trip was mind-blowing. Beautiful waters, beautiful forest, the river paralleled a train rail for a while and even crossed paths with the Appalachian Trail. A bald eagle followed us for a ways down the river, very patriotic and the rapids were epic.

We had a bit of rocky start... Mom kept getting in trouble by the guide. This whitewater rafting trip was way more involved than our last. On our trip down the Arkansas River, our guide would holler out a few commands on how we should paddle, but ultimately, he was the one controlling the ship, keeping us out of danger.

This trip was different. Everyone had their job on this raft. We were all responsible for keeping it on the straight, and sometimes, very narrow. We were all having such a great time, we couldn't help but get distracted by the adrenaline rush of the wave, and therefore couldn't help not paddling sometimes. Mom was laughing so hard and doing her best to stay in the small raft she abandoned paddling all together. Our guide was getting so frustrated telling her over and over to paddle, Lisa and I had to step in and finally say "woman, you gotta job to do!"

After we got in a rhythm though, we had a blast! Dipping, dodging, rolling with the waves, in and around boulders, through narrow slots in the rocks, it was brilliant! We managed to all stay in our raft too. Not even a close call like in Colorado.

I cannot say the same for the other raft. At one point we hear a loud scream, some splashing, and a bunch of laughing coming from behind us. The mother had fallen overboard on one of the rapids and she was now floating alongside the raft trying to pull herself back in. With no help from the daughter either, she was too busy laughing at the whole scene.

Karma is a wonderful thing though. Not 20 minutes later the daughter goes flying out of the raft through a section of rapids.

"Ain't so funny now, is it!?" we hear from the other raft as the guide and the mother pull her back in.

We decided to leave Banner Elk a day early and spend our actual last day of vacation in Asheville, NC. Which is also where we flew into and out of. This is a fun city to visit, even with the short amount of time we had here. Walking around, no plans, just exploring was a great day. Malaprop's Bookstore, Woolworth Soda Fountain, and the Mast General Store were just a few of our favorite finds.

The Biltmore Estate is what really attracted us to staying in Asheville for a night. This massive castle-like structure will amaze you from first glance. Well over one hundred years old, this massive mansion will leave you speechless with its 250 rooms, including a giant library, an indoor pool, and a huge pipe organ, because ... why not. So many intricate details, throughout every corner, donning every fireplace, it really is a beauty to see.

The best part in my opinion and absolutely shouldn't be skipped is the gardens. The Rose Garden, the Azalea Garden, the Walled Garden, even the Shrub Garden. So many different beautiful flora to see, all dripping with colors; purples, reds, yellows, pinks, whites. Your eyes almost can't take it all in.

After a great vacation, we headed back home. Asheville to Atlanta, Atlanta to St. Louis. Mom had made us "snackle-boxes" to take on the plane, and herself one of course. Everyone should get themselves a "snackle-box" for any trip, or have your mommy make you one like I did.

I was too full from dinner to eat any of mine, but I noticed she had hers on her tray at all times. Eating one jellybean at a time, very slowly. I was puzzled at first until I hear the stewardess say, "Ma'am, can you please put your mask back on?"

To which my mother replied, "Oh, I will after I eat my snack." Pops another jellybean. 467 miles later, she is still working on the jellybeans. My mother, ladies and gents.

That request seems a bit unnecessary now, the very next morning after our flight landed back in St. Louis, the mandatory masks on airplanes ceased. They couldn't have done that a day earlier??

Oh, and in case you are wondering... I did not see one single bear in the wild on this trip.

Not. A. One.

Chapter 21
Maui, HI

The year 2023 brought a couple of great celebrations. With that comes a great adventure.

Ever since Colorado, Emily had been planning her own graduation trip, knowing her time was just around the corner. Her only real request was one destination, she did have a few other places in mind as a backup because she knew this was a big ask.

Hawaii.

That is what she wanted most, so we made it happen. She would be graduating in May of '23, so we planned a trip for spring break of that year. With it being such a "big deal" trip, not just a simple drive a few states over, this would require a lot more planning, a lot more money, and a lot more days off. Lisa asked Em and Issy if this could be a dual graduation trip. Issy would be graduating the following year in May of '24. They both said absolutely. Anything to be able to go on this once in a lifetime trip. We also made this girls only trip. Combining our annual mother daughter trip with the now dual graduation trip. Me, Mom, Lisa, Em, and Issy would all be flying out to Maui for nine days of fun in the sun. One of the most magnificent trips we have ever taken.

We flew out super early. Like, Em didn't even go to bed yet early. Lisa had made us matching shirts for our trip; she, Mom, and I loved them. (Yes, I'm one of those nerds but I come by it honest) Emily and Issy promptly covered up with hoodies. Guess they weren't as keen on matching as we were.

I expected to be anxious about the flight. This would be the first flight traversing an ocean for all of us. Thousands of miles, with nothing but the Pacific beneath us, for anyone who has seen *Lost* or *Castaway*, it would be natural to be bothered by that. Much to my surprise, it really is no different than flying over land, other than the only thing you can see is clouds, blue sky, and blue ocean, lots of blue. The one thing I would say that was bothersome, would be sitting in a plane seat for eight hours straight! The tush will get very uncomfortable after a while.

The awesomeness of flying into Vegas during the night, was as tenfold flying into Maui during the day. Surrounded by nothing but sky and ocean, all of a sudden green mountains peak up into view. The impeccably contrasted deep blue ocean to vibrant green hills, a perfect welcome to a beautiful island.

We got ourselves a condo in Maalaea, right on the beach. It wasn't the Hilton, it wasn't in the prime shopping district, but it was perfect. We watched waves roll in every evening and the most incredible sunrises every morning from the comfort of our balcony. I could not have dreamed a more perfect view for our nine day stay. One of my favorite things was getting up early to see the sunrise over a clear view of Haleakalā, cup of coffee in hand and just the gentle sounds of the waves hitting the beach not ten feet away.

I've said one corner of heaven looks like Zion, the other I would bet looks like this.

Our first day was very chill. We wanted a lay of the land, to explore with no rules. So, we did just that. Exploring the area around our new home away from home and driving around looking for a place to stock up on food for the week. We loaded up our Jeep at the local grocery, (yeah, we rented a Jeep, I highly recommend), with stuff for lunch and local snacks to try. Also, we had to get reef safe sunscreen, which is possibly the worst type of sunscreen ever made. Its only, and I mean only, benefit is that it is safe for the environment. Elmers's Glue absorbs into the skin better than reef safe sunscreen, and probably protects the skin just as well, because the Pacific sun showed me no mercy and burnt me to a crisp on our very first day.

We had decided we would pack a lunch, but have dinner at a local restaurant each night. So many things to choose from, we had a blast picking something different every day. That was an experience itself. Fresh sushi was a must. It was by far our favorite, well Lisa, Issy, and I. Fresh fish and local dishes were our top priority to try. So much culture can be seen in a meal. The way it's prepared and served by locals with local ingredients, should be something everyone tries while away from home. Spam Musubi, Saimin, fresh sushi, acai bowls, fresh fruit and of course shaved ice were just some of the amazing local eats. With very different ingredients, yes, I mean the Spam, we were introduced to some very unique tastes, most we loved and some not so much.

In one instance I had to enjoy eating my words. I thought acai bowls were just some bougie teenager fad. I poked fun at the teenagers for saying we had to get them while in Hawaii. I gave it a chance and stole a bite of Ems. Well, I'm here to admit I was quick to judge, and they were delicious. I even ordered one for myself. Also, in case you were curious; Spam made the "love" column, I definitely recommend the Spam Musubi for breakfast.

On our first night we drove the beautiful Honoapiilani Highway toward Lahaina. Just the drive was amazing. Not in some super adrenaline inducing, high speed, roller coaster type way. It was just so beautiful and colorful, no matter if you looked out toward the ocean or up toward the mountains, we were surrounded by grandeur. Large tropical trees created a tunnel as we looped our way throughout the island passing locals heading for a surf or closing down the fruit stand. It was enchanting.

Lahaina is the perfect coastal town, with the main strip, Front Street, mere feet from the ocean. Full of shops and restaurants, frozen treats and souvenirs, all right there with the Pacific Ocean in sight. We chose Lahaina Fish Co. for our first dinner on the island. Mostly for its location, we were seated outside near the water to watch the most vibrant sunset I had ever seen. Colors of violet, sapphire, and coral were just a few of the shades that streaked across the sky. We sat there after dinner just in awe of where we were, looking out at the water, at Lanai and Kahoolawe Islands in view, and at the most brilliant colors of skyline I have ever witnessed.

After each of our trips, we like to play a game. "What was your favorite thing?" Sometimes the answers are all different. Sometimes they are all the same. Sometimes there is no possible way to pick just one thing.

That was this trip.

We packed so much into these nine days, not wanting to miss one single experience. Every day had something big, with your typical exploring thrown in too.

I would say that one adventure that was at the top of everyone's favorite list was snorkeling. We snorkeled Molokini Crater and Turtle Town with Makena Coastal Charters. I cannot recommend them enough. The group was small, the guides were patient and knowledgeable, and we had the absolute best time. We left the mainland behind early in the morning to hopefully be one of the first boats at the crater. The crater itself is away from the mainland of Maui a bit, nestled between the islands of Maui and Kaho'olawe. It is a partially submerged volcanic crater, that I hoped would still be a silent landmark while we were there.

We hopped out of the boat to spy on the marine life around us. Y'all, this was the most brilliant water I have ever been in. The clearest of clear and yet somehow still so beautifully blue. I felt like I was in an aquarium! Fish so bright and vibrant swam around us, not bothered at all by our presence. Yellow ones so bright they almost glowed, friendly black ones that would swarm around you just daring you to try and catch them. Blue, silver, purple, yellow, fish I've only seen in *Finding Nemo*. My eyes were unable to take it all in.

The tour then took us to an even more beautiful area, aptly named Turtle Town. This little corner of the ocean was spectacular. Less populated with fish this little area was home to so many Sea Turtles! This was a much better sighting than our experience in Mexico. These gentle ocean giants, swam lazily around, sometimes coming close to where we floated, but not overstaying their welcome. As a protected species you are not allowed to touch or chase them, but some of the turtles never got that message and would curiously swim right up next to you. It was an unbelievable dip in the ocean, and I would have gladly done it every day of our trip.

There was one very unexpected part about this whole excursion. It wasn't the sights, or the feel of the water, or the taste of the ocean. It was the sounds. While submerged, swimming through the crystal waters, I had ditched the floating devices long before, channeling my inner mermaid, I kept hearing a very distinct squeaking sound. Like Styrofoam cups rubbing together or the sides of a boat bumping against a dock but longer and more drawn out. It was only audible under the water though. So naturally, I assumed it did have something to do with the boat. I was so happily wrong.

The melodic squeal we heard under the water, it was a whale! Well, actually multiple whales, from miles away! This stunning sound was so mind-blowing. High pitched, perfectly in tune, song like. It was an unreal and rare experience.

It was birthing season for the North Pacific Humpback Whale, so these massive and beautiful creatures were seen and now heard throughout our entire trip. We had decided to take a whale watching tour after a long beach day. Something to relax and chill, while still exploring. It was a great tour. The whales breached the water's surface all over that channel between islands. They put on a show all afternoon, rising out of the water and splashing down to show how powerful they were, to gently raising a pectoral fin as if to give us a wave, to giving us a glimpse of their unique tail patterns while they gave it a flip out of the water.

As great as the whale watching tour was, it did not match the snorkeling tour. Seeing the beautiful marine life while submerged in the cool ocean waters, not only seeing but having the unique experience of listening to the call of the whales from insane distance away, is not something that can be repeated on your average snorkel trip. The weather had to be right, the timing had to be right, and the location had to be right. To say we were blessed with this once in a lifetime experience would be an understatement.

Along with snorkeling, there are so many other water activities to enjoy. We witnessed kayakers, paddleboarders, surfers, wind surfers, and so much more. Knowing how much we love kayaking and paddleboarding, we decided we should add that to the list of to-dos. Lisa came up with the idea we should rent a couple for the week. We had waterfront access from our condo and there are public beaches aplenty. So, we settled on renting paddleboards in hopes they were easier to transport.

Best idea ever.

We paddleboarded all over the Maalaea Bay. Up and down the beach, out toward deeper waters, getting braver each time out venturing farther and farther from the coast. We took them out to Kamaole Beach Park in nearby Kihei. Standing on the elongated surf boards you get quite the view to watch fish, jellyfish, and sea turtles swim under or near you.

While on these boards though we did have one situation. We have jokingly named it "The Big Accident". The waves were pretty relaxed the majority of our time here. Only while at Kamaole Beach did the waves get a little intense. This is not where "The Big Accident" happens though. Outside of our condo the ocean waves gently lapped the beach, lightly folding over themselves to get to the sand. Nothing a toddler couldn't handle walking along the shore in. This is where "The Big Accident" does happen.

Outside our condo the shoreline was a mixture of rocks and sand. Nothing you couldn't walk barefoot in, just had to be mindful of where you were and of the Sea Urchins that had set up camp in the crevasses of the lava rock. We had been at the beach all day, enjoying swimming, snorkeling, baking in the sun, and for the teenagers making TikTok's and having photo shoots. We were getting down to the last few hours we had with our paddleboards we rented, enjoying every last minute we could. Mom and I took them out for one last tour around the bay. Once again, the waves were very chill. We both were able to stand up on the boards, looking like we were well seasoned paddlers.

After heading down the coast as far as we dared, we headed back toward the condo and where the remainder of our team was camped out. Out in front, I would periodically turn my head, just enough to not throw myself off balance, making sure Mom was right behind me. She can go rogue sometimes. All seemed fine... then I hear...

"Amber!! I'm going surfing!!"

I turn my head around just in time to see an ill-timed wave and Mom's paddleboard parallel with it. In slow motion I watch Mom try to ride out this wave like Kelly Slater, fail, and tumble sideways into the ocean. Paddleboard rolls over top of her, the only thing keeping it from crashing into the beach is the ankle strap hooked to Mom.

I try to turn my board around as fast as I can, not an easy task, and paddle toward her in fear that she may be hurt. She did just have surgery only a couple months before this trip. When she surfaces from the water, well more like she turned herself upright, the water was barely three foot deep, she is howling with laughter. While relieved she didn't hurt herself, I also started giggling at the sight of Mom thinking she could surf on the paddleboard. Distracted with laughter I didn't see the now rogue wave coming straight for me as well. I also tumble end over end, landing pinky toe first against the rocks dotting the beach. My paddleboard also doing parkour across my back and skull.

Fishing ourselves off of the ocean floor, we wrestle back onto our paddleboards. Both chuckling at our ridiculous turn of events, from a relaxing jaunt across the bay to a scene from *America's Funniest Home Videos*. Lisa is standing on the edge of the beach, camera in hand. Waiting for either the next big shot or to come to our rescue.

Both Mom and I, were bruised a bit from the sudden tumble, and my poor pinky toe had seen better days. It was definitely worth every penny renting those boards.

Issy's one request while we were here, if possible, was to take surfing lessons. Since I survived "The Big Accident" I figured it would be a fun experience. Fun doesn't even scratch the surface.

I am pretty sure I am meant to live near the ocean. There is no water sport I won't try, well maybe swim with sharks, but even that isn't even a definite no.

Issy and I were the only ones of our team that went to surf school. The other three either didn't want to or tried to say they were "too old". Age is just a number fam.

We met up with Surf Club Maui in Kihei and our surfing instructor for some dry land lessons at Kalama Park. Which was very necessary. Our group of 6 were lined up with "long boards" in the middle of the park, getting instructions on how to lay on the board, paddle out, when to take off and when to spring up, stand, and surf. We looked like some crazy yoga class, but it would be all worth it when we got out to the water. The instructions we got on land seemed pretty cut and dry. Paddle out, go with the wave, bounce to a stand, and ride the wave to the beach.

In theory that's exactly how that should have gone. In reality, it wasn't quite like that. My weak arms couldn't paddle fast enough to stay in the wave, and the balance was not so easily mastered in the Pacific Ocean. Issy and I tried and failed so many times to stay up long enough to ride the wave to the beach. With the patience of our instructor and a lot of practice runs... like a lot of practice runs, we finally managed to get up. Riding the waves long enough to get some good photos, giving a shaka, tongue out like we really knew what we were doing, feeling like real surfers.

If you are water creatures like us, put this on the list, it was a blast. Memories to share with your kids, family, friends... or your niece, that they or you won't forget!

We wrapped up our day of surfing lessons doing one of the most Hawaiian things possible. A Luau! We all got dressed up in a tropical way. Adorned our hair with Hibiscus flowers donned our bracelets made of coconut shells and headed out to enjoy a night of Hula and Polynesian dance and delicious foods made famous by the island. Grass skirts, flowered lei's, shell necklaces, fire dancers. All of it was so mesmerizing, the Hawaiian and Polynesian culture has so much to explore. The food was delicious!

Myths of Maui put on an incredible show that night, enjoyable for folks of all ages! We got to learn, eat, and dance the night away. Treat yourself to a night of culture, great food, and a beautiful Hawaiian tradition. You won't regret it.

Another must do that made our list was the ever-popular Road to Hana. Thanks to a recommendation from a friend, we had a specific destination in mind on our road trip, other than enjoying the drive itself.

I had considered this a lazy activity day. One that didn't require a lot of stress or effort. Just a simple drive around the island. Enjoying the scenic landscape and beautiful waters of the Pacific and numerous streams that cascade down the mountain side. That's not exactly how it went.

The beautiful countryside of North Maui did not disappoint. Ocean views filled our windows with that unique deep blue, the green jungle filled the other windows, sometimes making a tunnel of greenery sending us into a real-life version of *Fern Gully*.

However, the drive was not what we had expected. Only 43 miles separate Ho'okipa Beach Park (where *we* considered the start of The Road to Hana) and the town of Hana. Google says that should take you a little less than two hours. It took us every bit of three. Hairpin turns, blind corners, one lane bridges, the road zigzags more than an EKG reading.

With white knuckles most of the time, I drove the entire 43 miles. Only getting yelled at a couple of times by the passenger's for coming too close to the edge or too close to the other cars. Mostly the complaints were the speed of our travel, all for different reasons. Lisa and Em were getting car sick, Issy was being crushed in the middle seat every turn, and Mom simply wanted to be able to look at everything.

Road issues aside, the day was incredible. The Road to Hana had plenty of places to pull over, to either check out the panoramic views, hike a trail, or simply recover from the series of 180 degree turns. Hawaiian Monk

Seals laid on the rocks at Ho'okipa Beach Park, incredible flowers from Birds of Paradise to Hibiscus to Parakeet Flowers were on every hiking trail, waterfalls big and small cascaded down the hillside, unbelievable sights were around every hairpin turn.

My favorite section of the entire road, the Eucalyptus Rainbow Trees. These gargantuan timbers are unlike anything you will ever see in the Midwest, or heck probably anywhere else in the country. These are more than just trees. These are paintings. Colorful and rare, even mesmerizing. How can a simple tree trunk be so unique? Pinks, reds, the brightest green, if you look long enough you may even start to see other colors. Not only do the incredible colors strike you, but the insane size will have you in awe.

Although the road was a vomit inducing, white knuckle roller coaster, it was an incredible treat to witness all the different sights from just one section of this small island.

Our end goal on this insane road trip was no slouch either. Wai'ānapanapa State Park. (Don't ask me how to pronounce that.) Although not a free state park, and reservations are required, it is completely worth it. Worth the crazy drive to get there and the $16 to get in. The beach is unreal. Very emo. Made completely of jet black sand, you will feel as though you have left earth entirely and have been transported to another world (if you haven't felt that way already from the drive in). Volcanic rock line the coast and dense forest surrounds the beach, putting you in perfect solitude away from the city and the traffic.

Try not to burn your feet on the sweltering black sand and dive in, because the crystal-clear waters are picturesque and full of marine life. Fish are everywhere, as many as when snorkeling Molokini Crater darting around and playing hide and seek, and of course Sea Turtles can't wait to play a game of "can't touch me!".

The beach and park were amazing. The drive in, though stressful was beautiful and breathtaking. Road to Hana is a staple when visiting Maui and for good reason. Things seen on this stretch of highway are so insanely unique to the island and our beautiful country itself. Don't miss it, even if you can't make it all the way to Hana, get just a sample of a drive because it is well worth it.

One of our last adventures on the island was quite the doozy, made up of more mishaps than not, it was still a good time and made for some pretty fun memories.

Haleakalā National Park.

As mentioned before, we have become somewhat the National Park junkies. So, we of course couldn't leave this incredible island without visiting one of the major National Parks here.

Haleakalā has two options for visiting. Sunrise or Sunset. Obviously, you can visit in-between of those times too but those are the main options. Sunrise requires reservations but it's only $1.50. Sunset is free.

We of course choose the sunrise option. Because who doesn't love getting up early on vacation. I mean I love getting up early. I work nightshift so I never have to get up early. Mom wanted the sunrise view though, and Mom gets what Mom wants. Plus, it did seem like a pretty cool idea, watching the sunrise from the top of a volcano.

We got up and left around 3am, the drive would take over an hour and we wanted to make sure we got a good spot to view the sun rising over the Red Hill. Thank God it was still dark when we entered the dozens of switchbacks in the highway, or it would have been Pikes Peak all over again. This drive did come with a few gasps whenever the headlights would illuminate the sheer drop-offs. Mostly from Lisa, but she did only grab at my arm once or twice. Growth.

Something I did not realize until we were on our 14th switchback up the road, was that we should have fueled up before we left. I was alerted to that fact by the blinking low fuel light on the dash. I tried to keep this information to myself, while mentally thinking about what we would do if we ran out of gas. We were less than halfway up the steep mountain, and we still would have to make it back down and to the nearest town, that wasn't exactly close, before we could fill up. I pocketed that problem for later, thinking that my walk to the gas station would be a scenic one at least.

After our second thrilling road trip this vacation, we've made it to the top of Haleakalā, and just in time to get great 'seats' near the Pa Ka'oao Trail.

Something we weren't quite prepared for.... The weather. This is an island vacation. Sun, sand, ocean, hot, hot, hot. However, the top of this mountain was not hot, hot, hot. It was definitely cold, cold, cold. Thankfully we each had brought a hoodie and had thrown a couple of blankets in the back of the car. It wasn't enough though. We all huddled together arguing over who had more of the blanket, each of us pulling and tugging trying to get just an inch more property of this warmth.

Not only was it colder than we were expecting, but we were also lucky enough to have it rain on us while we were up in elevation. How it was not snowing is beyond me, because, it certainly felt cold enough to do so. We patiently waited for the rain and clouds to clear, anticipating the sunrise, and the golden rays over the volcano, anxiously wanting to see the beautiful scene it would display and desperately seeking its warmth. We waited, and waited, and waited some more. Now officially drenched, freezing, and annoyed, we'd come to the conclusion that we have missed the sunrise views due to rain clouds. What. A. Bummer. We woke up before the sun, so that we could see the sun, and now we can't see the sun.

Frustrated, cold, wet, and hungry, we head back to the car, but we don't leave just yet. We decide to give the sun a bit of time to dry up the cloud cover. We wanted to get in at least a small hike to view the volcano but didn't want to do that inside of a rain cloud. Also, the gift shop wasn't open yet so obviously we are waiting for that. So instead of taking off back down the hill, we opted for quick power naps in the Jeep.

Our trip to the National Park was kind of a bust. We did get some epic views of the dormant volcano after the sun had risen, and also of the island below as well. Even though the sunrise view didn't go as planned we still had a great time and marked one more National Park off our bucket list.

There was, however, one more hurdle to this disastrous trip to Haleakalā. The gas tank. As we pulled out of the Visitor Center headed down the mountain and the umpteen switchbacks, the dashboard lights up once again informing my dumbass that I forgot to fuel up before we left.

An idea hits me as we are heading down a decent incline. I shift into neutral and ride the brakes and fumes to the bottom. Issy catches my movement, and curiously asks "are you not in gear??". To which I have to admit to the team that no, I am not, and we are nearly out of gas with 17 miles to the nearest station. I got quite a few remarks from that statement but in the end it all worked out. My big plan worked, and we coasted all the way to the Texaco.

Nothing totally horrible happened to us while on this trip. Some ridiculousness, yes, and a few mishaps, of course. What would one of our trips be without that... we obviously wouldn't know - we've never had a trip without at least one goofy thing or another. But all in all, it was a pretty nontraumatic trip....

For us.

For those visiting a few months later, the same could not be said.

It saddens me now thinking about visiting Lahaina. How beautiful, vibrant, and full of life the coastal town was. How much we enjoyed walking the streets, enjoyed the people and the experience, not knowing less than five months later Lahaina would be nothing but memories. Turned into a desolate corner of the island by a destructive and fast spreading fire. Our most favorite city while on the island is now no more, lost are the beautiful buildings, the friendly coastal atmosphere, and the over 100 people who perished. Though we are not Hawaiian natives, just another set of tourists that fell in love with a beautiful island and culture, we were devastated that day when the news broke about the destruction. We mourned for the people and prayed for the city, in hopes they could feel the love from our little corner of Missouri.

To say we loved Hawaii would be an understatement. The food, the feels, the lifestyle, we couldn't get enough of it. The mood was relaxed-always. The rich history was on every corner. So many things to try and explore. Colors even seemed brighter, more vibrant somehow. All on this one tiny island. I said it was a once in a lifetime trip. I sincerely hope that isn't true. Hawaii left a mark on my soul. I will forever be ready for a return trip.

Maybe I should go back to school for something so we can have another graduation trip to this remarkable island.

Chapter 22
Gatlinburg, TN

Family vacation. We are back again. The whole fam-damily. Although this one is different from the last few, no cruise and not at Christmas time. We, as usual had a blast, and as usual, there were many ups and downs the whole week. One event in particular that, although I didn't know it then, would end up changing my life forever.

This year's family fun destination is Gatlinburg, Tennessee and The Great Smoky Mountains. A week of fun and adventure with, count them, twelve people! Twelve! Our circle sure has grown a lot over the years.

It takes somewhere between eight and nine hours for us to get to that part of Tennessee. Which of course had to include time to stop at the famous Buc-ee's gas station. Traversing an area we are very familiar with, crossing into Kentucky via Illinois toward Mom's new home near Kentucky Lake. So, we figured since we are driving right by, we'll just swing by and pick her up on the way! Although she couldn't stay the entire week, she did follow the convoy to spend a couple of days with us, enjoying the beautiful scenery and hunting bears of course!

With a camera... don't be silly.

We wanted to visit Great Smoky Mountains National Park, that was a must on our to do list. We also had plans of checking out downtown Gatlinburg, souvenir shopping, maybe some regular shopping, swimming at the resort, and of course celebrating Lisa's birthday!

We spent day one in town. At a fun place called Anakeesta, a theme park that can be reached by ski lift. This park is full of things to do for everyone, sitting at the top of a mountain right in downtown Gatlinburg. If not a fan of ski lifts there is an option of taking the shuttle bus to the top, we however all choose to take the lifts.

Observation tower, dueling zip lines, shops, giant bird houses, a skywalk, mountain coasters. There really is so much to do here, for the young and old. Unfortunately, the day we went all other tourists in Gatlinburg also decided it would be fun, so it was crowded and we waited forever in sweltering heat of summer, but it was still an enjoyable day.

We headed up to the observation tower, getting 360° of panoramic mountain views. Incredible views of the Smokies, with that classic haze stretched out in every direction. Signs around the deck gave you directions on what you may be able to see on a clear day, identifying the various mountains in the far-off distance. On a clear day, you might even see Kentucky.

Another favorite spot was the Treetop Skywalk. Like a big kid's treehouse, with hundreds of feet of rope bridges hovering over the earth below, weaving in and around trees on these hanging bridges, can make you feel like a kid on a playground again. Especially when the college football player decides to wait until his 'afraid of heights' mother is right in the middle before jumping and thrashing the bridge all over the place. It was truly a sight to see, watching a woman yell at her 23-year-old 6'5" son. I assure you, he was very terrified.

Anakeesta was a fun day, and had we had more time and less heat we would have been able to take advantage of the entire park but trying to wrangle 12 people in one spot just isn't easy.

The favorite part of the day, well for about half the group anyway, was the ski lift down. This is where our first bear encounter happens. While heading down, a small Black Bear was spotted walking under the ski lift toward the tree line. I was not privileged enough to get to see it, but 5 out of the 12 did. The remainder of us will just have to be on alert for our chance to see the famous Black Bears of the Smokies.

While Anakeesta wasn't my favorite part of Gatlinburg, mostly because I didn't get to see the bear, downtown does have a lot to offer. Shops, restaurants, souvenirs, ice cream, and of course, in the heart of Tennessee – moonshine.

To escape the heat, I recommend swinging through Ripley's Aquarium, and/or The Crazy Mason Milkshake Bar. We chose both, it was just so hot!

Ripley's is your typical aquarium, fish, sharks, octopi- oh my! However, it does have a lot to offer for being smack in the middle of a bustling downtown tourist area. A mermaid show throughout the day, a moving pathway through an underwater tunnel giving you a unique view to some beautiful and sometimes scary creatures, plus it is full of interactive activities for the little ones on the team.

The Crazy Mason Milkshake Bar is an ice cream shop on steroids. What all children's ice cream dreams are made of. It has something for everyone. Chocoholics, peanut butter freaks, fruity fans, and something a little crazy for the oddballs.

Both of those are highly recommended by all of our team, especially the 2- and 4-year-olds.

The grown-ups of the group enjoyed a break from the heat in other shops. Tennessee Cider Company, Sugarlands Moonshine Distillery,

Ole Smoky Distillery "The Barrelhouse", and Ole Smoky Distillery "The Holler", just to name a few. Those ways to beat the heat come highly recommended by those 21 and over.

There is one thing Tennessee is not short on, and that is alcohol. In a wide variety of proof, flavors, and forms. Moonshine, whiskey, hard cider, wine, something called sipping cream, which was new to me, all can be found in a quarter mile strip of downtown Gatlinburg.

Make sure you take yourself a DD or grab an Uber because even though it's just a "tasting", it's moonshine, a little goes a looooonnnng way my friends.

Our home away from home this trip was Bluegreen Vacations Mountain Loft Resort. With 12 people in our crew, we had to take up multiple rooms, our people were scattered everywhere.

The resort is conveniently located off highway 321. Away from the noise of the city, but still within just a few minutes of all your favorite tourist stops. Also handy was the fact that it was 4-minute drive from the nearest grocery. When there are 12 in the group, something is always needed. Vacation bologna, birthday candles, baby Tylenol for when the 2-year-old went Ronda Rousey on the 4-year-old, (yeah, she's kind of mean, or "misunderstood" as my sister calls it), bottled water, more vacation bologna, and Starbucks.

The craziest thing though. Less than 2 months after our vacation, a land slide occurred on that grocery store's property. Taking out an entire retaining wall and covering the parking lot with mud and debris from the adjoining hillside. Another natural disaster?? Yeah, we are going to end up on some kind of vacation watchlist if these natural disasters don't stop happening after we leave.

The resort is top notch. Even with 12, we had plenty of room, our own kitchens, multiple pools and hot tubs to pick from, and our own mini golf course. Since it was tucked back in the forested mountain side, I hoped and waited my chance to see a black bear every time I went outside. I quietly snuck around outside when heading to the pool or hot tub, or even taking the trash out, just for one glimpse at those furry beasts.

One night after celebrating Lisa's birthday with a homemade cake and an incorrect number of candles, my phone buzzes "Get to the pool now!" it was from Mad Dog. "There is a huge black bear by the pool!!"

The remainder of us that are still cleaning up the birthday celebration sprint down to the pool, and for some of us, we were excited to see our first bear of the trip.

"Wow! That was so cool!"

"Did you see? It was so close!"

"That was awesome!"

Those were the conversations going around the pool when we got there from the other guests, Mad Dog, and her friend.

We, however, missed it!! All of us that went down to the pool, waited for it to come back until it closed, but no luck. Chance number two to see black bears was now also a bust.

Fine. We are going to the National Park tomorrow. We'll see a bear there for sure!

Our first venture into Great Smoky Mountain National Park was also moms last day of vacation with us. She had to get back to her patients in Kentucky.

After a bit of research, we decided on Cades Cove area of the park.

Gatlinburg is like the front door to Great Smoky Mountains National Park. One second you are driving on a popular city strip with crowds going in and out of restaurants and shops, next thing you know you are surrounded by the beautiful scenes of wilderness.

GSMNP is known to be the most visited National Park in the United States. I don't know exact numbers but it sees millions of visitors annually. For good reason, centrally located, near huge tourist destinations of Gatlinburg and Pigeon Forge, and it boasts of beautiful mountain landscapes, numerous hiking trails, and amazing history.

We had to stop at the Sugarland Visitor Center first, obviously. Not just so I can spend all of my money on things that have National Park plastered all over it, you are also required to have a parking permit to hang out in GSMNP. Which was ironic because we couldn't even find a parking spot at the visitor center to get our parking pass. Not surprising since it is one of the most visited parks around.

All three cars split up in search of an inch of land to pull into. Brenden stuck their car in between a couple of SUVs near the woods, Em managed to find a legal vacant spot, and I pulled Mom's car off on the shoulder, parking right next to a sign that said, "NO PARKING". Like so close I couldn't even play the "*I didn't see it*" card, because I had to avoid hitting it with my car door when I got out. I wasn't worried, there were people pulled over everywhere abandoning their vehicles in the most obscure places to go in the visitor center.

So, money spent, parking pass bought, parking ticket avoided, we were off to Cades Cove.

This section of the park is on the western side. It's full of hiking, wildlife, amazing photo backdrops, and lots of historic buildings. Its main feature is an 11-mile loop road, taking you through and around some amazing views of the park. Old cabins, historic churches, cemeteries, are just a few of the staples here. And guess what friends! There is a Cades Cove Visitor Center. You'll be so proud though, I didn't buy anything here, I didn't even go in. I think we all know by now I would have bought the lot if I had gone in.

Our trip around wasn't without its troubles. We weren't even halfway around the loop when the car of teenagers informs us that the gas light is on. Not this again. Apparently, that's our new thing. Don't check the gas gauge before leaving civilization. This wouldn't be as easy to get around as our gas troubles in Hawaii, this was not some place you could just coast downhill. There was no need for panic that ensued from that car though, we made it to the station without having to push.

Cades Cove was beautiful. The Primitive Baptist Church, the Methodist Church, and the Missionary Baptist Church were undoubtedly my favorites. The Dan Lawson Cabin ranks high as well. Each church had its own corresponding cemetery. If you are lucky, you can be at the Primitive Baptist Church while there is a Ranger stationed, giving some history and answering questions about the area.

Another key feature to Cades Cove is the Cades Cove Overlook. Full of wildflowers, wildlife, and unobstructed views of the Smokies. It was here that we were all but guaranteed to see bears. I was excited, every stump and pile of brush I was sure it was a bear. The entire drive I was practically hanging out the window, waiting for a bear to come into view.

Ask me how many bears we saw at Cades Cove... ask me.

NONE!

Chance number 3 another strike. Fine. We still have days left, we'll see one in the park tomorrow, no doubt.

Our next adventure into GSMNP was to Clingmans Dome. Mom had to take off back to Kentucky after Cades Cove, so we were down to only 11 in the crew now.

Clingmans Dome, now referred to as Kuwohi, sits on the Tennessee, North Carolina border and is the highest point in GSMNP. So, it promises to have some of the best views. We took the gorgeous and very picturesque drive from the very busy visitor center (had to get that parking pass), in awe at every turn through the mountains. It took us about an hour to get to the parking area of Clingmans Dome, but it was one of the best drives. Giant bends in the highway, trees opened up along the drive for you to be able to see the eerie haze that weaves around each peak, even in the dog days of summer, the mountains are still so Smoky.

The pride of Clingmans Dome is the observation tower. Boasting ridiculously awesome views, it's no wonder it's so popular. Its popularity may cause you to cruise the parking lot a few times searching for a spot, we had to anyway. No making something up to fit your car in, unless you want to risk careening down the mountain side. On the plus side, you get a few more opportunities for your car to win at the "licenses plate game".

Clingmans Dome also has its own visitor center like Cades Cove. Unlike Cades Cove, I did go into this one. I had to get my National Park Passport stamped. Yes, I spent more money. Don't judge.

The hiking trail to the observation tower is only a half mile or so, so we all felt like this was going to be a very easy stroll through the woods. The pathway is even paved. How hard could it be?

Answer. Very hard! This was one of the toughest most difficult hikes I have ever been on. Including my hike in Zion. Literally half of a mile, straight up. No flat spots, no switchbacks, nothing. Just point A to point B, vertical.

We finally hoof it all the way to the top of this literal mountain. Most exhausting half mile walk of my life. The views are breathtaking. Literally. I've seen the Rockies and I've seen white sand beaches, but there is just something about the Appalachian Mountain Range. Possibly because it makes me feel at home, the green, rolling Appalachian Mountains remind me so much of the green, rolling hills of the Ozark Mountains in Missouri. It feels so familiar and warm, I can't help but falling in love with this view.

Photo ops are everywhere. At over 6,000 feet of elevation, you can see for miles on a clear day. The dark mysterious blue mountains in the distance to the stark green hills below you, it is nature at its best.

Since you're so high up, you can also get a spot of cell service at the top of the observation tower.

This is where the mishap occurs, the not so good in the vacation.

Warning. Not all vacation mishaps are funny or comical. Some, well, some just really suck. Sometimes they change your life in ways that you never wanted.

At the top of Clingman's Observation Tower, I got just enough signal to receive a text. One text. One moment. Life changed.

Although the tower was full of people and families, enjoying the unique 360° views, I could only hear silence. My stomach drops when I read the message, and my heart begs my eyes to be wrong about what I just read.

It's from my best friend Katie, we met her in an earlier chapter. Her cancer had returned. It not only had returned, but it had returned with a vengeance and set up camp in both her lungs and her bones.

Katie had beaten cancer once already. She was diagnosed with a rare heart tumor called a Cardiac Angiosarcoma. She told me once, that a person has a higher chance of winning the lottery than getting this form of cancer. Well, she was that one in a million. She fought hard, and she beat it, so our lives were going back. Back to how they should be. Evenings on the back patio, pizza nights, closing down our favorite Mexican joint, making plans to buy land next to each other. Plans to build houses next to each other so that we could spend days on end at one or the others home like we did when we were kids. We had plans for vacations, traveling and exploring, and maybe even another cruise. Alaska, Hawaii, whatever- we were going.

That one simple text erased all of those plans.

Katie departed this earth not four months after I received that text message at the top of Clingmans Dome.

She fought with every ounce of her, she fought long and hard but with grace and bravery. I asked myself at the very end *why did I not recognize how bad it really was?* I realize now that it's because she wouldn't have let me. No matter what, she was always smiling when I saw her. Always had excitement in her voice when we talked on the phone, never once burdening me with the pain she was in. Never once showing any fear she may have been feeling. That's the kind of friend she was. Always making sure others were happy first.

I wept hard that day at the top of Clingmans Dome. Unaware of the heartbreak that I would suffer just a few months later. In a strange way The Great Smoky Mountains showed sympathy for me that day. On the way back down the mountain it began to rain, blending my salty tears with the sweet rain, the mountains showed us that they could be sad too.

I mean really sad too, because it rained so freaking hard!!

I don't include this part to make anyone sad, or for anyone to feel sorry for me. I include it because it's the truth, because it's real. While most mishaps in this book are funny, amusing, and mostly ridiculous, this one is painful and heartbreaking and like most our travels, life changing. A family vacation isn't the ideal place to find out that your best friend is dying of cancer. But it was exactly where I needed to be, surrounded by my support system, my team. Maybe that is why she choose to tell me then, so my family could be there to ease the pain. Shoulders to cry on, words of wisdom, hope, and support, and a bunch of goofballs trying to keep my mind off the details.

I cannot stress this enough. Take the trip. Go on the adventure. Splurge. Snap every photo. Make all the memories. As cliché as it is, you'll only regret the things you didn't get to do.

After I pulled myself together a little, well mostly my team pulled me together. We made our way back down the near vertical trail in the pouring rain. That trail is a hundred times easier on the way down by the way, even if it's during a downpour. On our drive back to the resort we got separated a bit. So, the car with everyone but me and the four teenagers in it pulled over to wait for us to catch up.

To recap, the only ones on this trip who haven't seen a bear are me, Mom, Em, Lisa, and The Doug. Mom never did get the chance to see one before she headed home.

We, me, Em, and the other teens, see the other car pulled over, and we idle up behind them. Lisa jumps out hustles over to our car.

"You just missed it!! A big ol' black bear just popped out of the brush over there! She walked around for a bit and then disappeared back into the woods! It was so cool!"

Well, that's just great.

Another bear. That I missed by mere moments. Em and I never did see a bear this trip. Maybe next time, or on some other adventure, but not in Blue Ridge Mountains and not in The Great Smoky Mountains.

I think God is just having fun with this now.

Chapter 23
St. Louis, MO

One day, in the summer of 2023, Mom came up for the weekend. It was a perfect summer day out, blue skies dotted with the occasional bright white cotton ball clouds, hot and humid like any summer day in Missouri, and all three of us were off of work, Lisa, Mom, and I.

It was this short trip that created this book. What should have been a simple short day to explore the city, put the "icing on the cake" as you might say, for me and all our ridiculous adventures.

After her three-ish hour drive to get to my house from Kentucky, Mom, as always, asks "So, what do we wanna do?". After listing off the possible options, we somehow landed on going to see the St. Louis Arch. We had all been before one time or another, whether from a school field trip or just another random day like this one. We hadn't been, however, since it was redesignated as a National Park. Ever since our venture to Zion, we have become National Park junkies.

Lisa stated the only way she was going is if we went somewhere good for lunch, more specifically The Old Spaghetti Factory on Laclede's Landing. That didn't require a lot of persuading from the two of us, so we headed out, opting for lunch first. I know what you might be thinking, *The Spaghetti Factory? That's not very original?* True, there are more unique and "St. Louis-y" restaurants than this Italian chain. This location is in the oldest district of St. Louis, Laclede's Landing, in a very historic building formerly known as the Christian-Peper Building. Plus, we have a lot of "fond" memories here, like the time Mom almost killed my new stepdad when he said Mom's lasagna wasn't real. Well, that's not exactly what he said but that's how we turned it around to make it sound like that's what he meant. All in good fun though.

When dinner was over, stuffed with pasta and spumoni, we go to order our tram tickets for The Gateway Arch online.

It's sold out!

The entire reason we came here was to visit The Arch and now it's sold out. Well crap. So, Lisa tries a different angle and calls the booking department for tickets. Not surprisingly the lady explains that they are in fact sold out just like the website says. She could, however, set us up with tickets for a riverboat tour, and of course The Arch grounds and museum are free and don't require reservations.

Like with so many journeys before, we settled for plan B.

Sometimes I believe The Arch gets a bad rap. On more than one occasion I have seen questions like "what can you even do there" or "is it even worth visiting". To that I say, of course it's worth visiting and there are plenty of things to do in and around this park. I get St. Louis isn't exactly on everyone's "bucket list", understandably so as it tends to flirt with the top spot-on America's most dangerous cities. Do I think you need an entire week here? No.

I do think it is worth a visit if given the chance, though.

We made our way to The Arch grounds from the cobblestone streets of Laclede's Landing and past the famous Eads Bridge. With beautiful views of the unruly muddy Mississippi, the well-manicured grounds offer plenty of photo ops, picnic spots, and places to just take a walk around the park. We grab our obligatory selfies with The Arch, bright blue sky as a perfect backdrop to the massive bend of steel towering over the city. The Midwest humidity and sun beating down on us had us feeling very sweaty and sticky in just a short amount of time, and since we had a bit before our riverboat tour started, we headed inside and underneath The Arch to check out the museum and to get in some much-needed air conditioning.

While museums aren't really my thing, it is worth a visit. The museum itself is huge, providing plenty of history about The Arch and the surrounding area. Plenty of displays to learn all about how St. Louis got started, the indigenous people who lived here first, and how The Arch itself was constructed. There is even a virtual theater and a model of one of the tram cars that take you to the top.

If claustrophobic, take a seat in the model car before risking a freakout climbing 630' up with no way to stop until you reach the top. If unsure if you are claustrophobic, take a seat in the model. That would be a bad time to find out about a fear you didn't know you had.

After we had our fill of the museum, we headed to one of our… okay one of *my*, favorite parts of National Parks. I'm sure you can guess it. The gift shop. Even though it is the smallest National Park, the gift shop is not. So many things to peruse; books, tee shirts, coffee cups, stickers, keychains, postcards. The amount of money I am capable of spending on souvenirs is slightly ridiculous. Did I mention this place is an hour from my house? It's not like I'm an actual tourist, but here I am in line with arms full.

As I am standing in line, waiting my turn behind the dozen or so other people, I notice a few things, and they aren't good things. The guy in front of me is buying an umbrella, the guy in front of him is buying two, the three people behind me all have one or more ponchos in hand to purchase. *Interesting,* I think to myself as I stand there with two new books and a coffee mug, *It was bright and shiny when we came in, what do these people know that I don't.*

We make our final purchases and head toward the exit to get to the riverboat for our tour. As we exit the doors marked in big giant letters "NO RE-ENTRY" we are met with...

KAA-POW.

A massive lightning bolt shoots across the now near black sky. Sharp cracks and low rumbles every second. Rain coming down so hard it's basically one giant sheet of water in constant flow from the skies above. Crashes of lightning and thunder are so close together you can't tell when one stops and the next begins. The steps leading out of The Arch are now flooded with rainwater, pouring in from the levels above.

The three of us just stand there, dumbfounded. Where the heck did our bright and shiny day go??

Now what?

We can't go back in, we would have to go back to the entrance, which would require walking through this now monsoon that is taking place. We obviously can't get to the car either, that is blocks away. We have 45 or so minutes before our boat tour. As we stand there like the Midwesterners we are, just watching it storm, it occurs to me that they might cancel the riverboats if it is lightning. So, I call...

"Oh yes, absolutely we are still going, we don't cancel for a *little* rain." She says to me, slightly snooty, like I was the ridiculous one.

Broad, have you looked outside? It's like freaking Jumanji *out here.* That's what I am thinking anyways, as I tell her "Great! Thanks! We'll be there."

It's now only 15 minutes until our departure time and the rain hasn't let up even a little. Well, better get going. We all three sprint up the steps, now a cascade of waterfalls, and run toward the riverfront. It takes less than a second for the three of us to become completely soaked. Shoes squishing with each step, Mom using her giftbag as an umbrella, the attempt was futile as her hair now sticks to her face. Lisa has had to stop multiple times to dig her flip flops out of the current of water surging down the sidewalk. I am dying with laughter as I think about how ridiculous we look. Soaked head to toe, make-up running down each of our faces, Lisa and I trying to protect our new souvenirs from the rain, Mom using her new souvenirs to protect herself from the rain.

Let's go to St. Louis she said, it'll be fun she said.

We finally make it through the downpour and into the gift shop at the boat dock. Wringing our clothes out the best we can, watching the others that also braved the flood waters. Lisa, Mom, and I make our way to the line forming around back to board the riverboat, and it is at that moment a member of the staff summons our attention.

"Folks... Folks...because of the storm we unfortunately will have to cancel the 4:45 tour. If you would like to exchange your ticket for a later departure time or get a full refund, please head inside.... Sorry for any inconvenience."

I am seething.

Mom and Lisa are looking at me, like *I thought we didn't cancel??*

Four forty-five comes and goes and no tour, even though the weather now really could be described as "a little rain".

While in line to get our refund, Lisa has me check to see if maybe there are some tickets available now for the tram ride to the top of The Arch. Hoping maybe some folks chickened out at riding to the top of a massive steel arch in a lightning storm.

Lucky for us, there must've been a few, because we had our pick of time slots for the evening. So, we ford our way back across the rain-soaked streets and sidewalks to the saturated Arch grounds, sloshing back into the front entrance of The Arch. Now slightly chilly from a combination of wet clothes and air conditioning, we go back to the gift shop for a dry shirt. It won't completely fix our "drowned rat" look we have going but it will make us feel marginally better about ourselves.

The storm let up at just the right time. Although the once perfect sunny day is now gone, the views from the top are as impressive as ever. Low clouds and fog now hug the high-rises of downtown St. Louis. The lush green of the park grounds stand out among the gray buildings. The evening sunset now just barely visible at the western edge through the clouds. Through the east side windows the chocolate-colored waters of the Mississippi meander along the banks at its usual pace, in no hurry whatsoever to get to New Orleans.

The day did not go as planned to say the least, heck not 24 hours earlier we had no plans at all. It worked out to be a great day though. We laughed, a lot. We got soaked, a lot. We had fun anyway, the day wasn't ruined by not getting to go to the top of The Arch, or by the monsoon, or by the canceled boat trip. All of that combined actually made for a pretty memorable day.

After our visit, we discuss how many National Parks we have now visited, and what's next on the list. Pondering on our adventures and how blessed we are. We have seen so many great things and have had some of the most ridiculous and unbelievable stories to tell when we get back from our adventures.

We make our way back to the car, everything still mostly wet except our new shirts, those are nice and dry, when a rain drop hits me in the face. Then another and then another. Then more just keep falling. Our once new dry shirts are now soaked, yet again. Mom is once again using her souvenirs to "block" the rain from reaching her already drenched curls. We don't even run this time. We just stop and take in the craziness of the day, and I yell at them both through the drizzle of water...

"And this is why we should write a book."

Epilogue

This is by no means the end of my adventures....

This is only the beginning. Currently, as I write these last few pages, I am making a packing list for my next big adventure...

Alaska!

With Katie's mom, dad, and sister.

Plan A was to go with Katie, but as usual I'll have to go with plan B. But I can't imagine a better plan B, or going to Alaska with anyone else. Our families, mine and Katie's.

My cousin once told me, "Grieve as long as you need, because there is no time limit on grief. Then... do something that makes them proud."

I hope this does just that.

Vacations change you. Travel and adventure changes you. You may not realize it in the moment, but it will change you. I wholeheartedly believe that.

It may not be an immediate effect like my trip to Zion, where I witnessed how beautiful this country truly is, forever in awe at what creations God has given us.

Or like my first trip to the Caribbean, a change that has put an imprint on my soul, causing an addiction to travel. An addiction that I hope to never be cured from.

Sometimes it's slow and the change happens afterwards, like the trip to The Great Smoky Mountains, a change that happened months after I returned home. A change that I am still trying to heal from.

Travel mishaps can happen in a variation of ways. From missing your flight to getting lost on the trail. Typical blunders in life. Or the non-typical problems like surviving a cruise ship crash, or being stuck in the Saint Francois Mountain range with nothing but a flashlight and a kayak at 2 AM. None of those things are the villains in the story, they are what make life interesting. They give character to your travel and to your adventure. Life is not perfect, so don't always count on your adventures to be either. Don't ever be afraid of the mishap, the detour, the wrong turn, the near miss, or even the full miss.

Sometimes those are the best parts of life.

By the way...That list I mentioned of places to try should be getting pretty long by now... you better get going...

Just watch out for the seagulls and other mishaps....

Acknowledgements

First and foremost, I want to thank God. Without His strength and wisdom, none of this would have been possible. I give Him all the glory for bringing me through every challenge and blessing in these stories, and for blessing me with the ability to share them.

To my family, my team, my friends: your love, humor, passion for travel, and need for adventure have been the base on which this book was built. Thank you for letting me tag along.

Specifically...

To my parents, thank you for teaching me the values of hard work, faith, and perseverance. Thank you for leading by example. And thank you for supporting me in anything I set out to do.

To my siblings, Lisa and Josh, thank you for your laughter, your kindness, your ability to keep me humble, and for always being there when I needed you most. Love you more!

To my nieces and nephews, thank you for simply existing and for the best title in the world. Thank you for "filling my cup", especially when I don't even realize it's empty. I love you all more than I could ever explain in words.

To my friends, whether you are in this book or not, I am deeply grateful for your friendship, your encouragement, laughter, and understanding. Thank you for getting me through one of the toughest years of my life.

To Heather, whose love for reading sparked my own, thank you for forcing me to read your favorite books, all of them, you opened the doors to a world of stories and imagination.

A special thank you to Cody Michael Mahurin for the stunning cover art that truly brought this book to life.

Lastly, to anyone who has crossed my path and contributed to this book, whether through inspiration, feedback, proofreading, or simply by being part of my life—thank you.

www.ingramcontent.com/pod-product-compliance
Lightning Source LLC
Chambersburg PA
CBHW020535030426
42337CB00013B/858